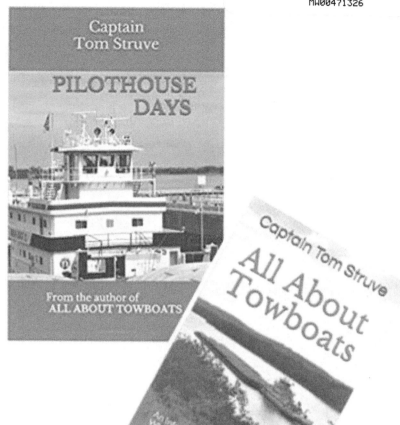

Deckhand Days

BY

Captain Tom Struve

BookworQs.com

APRIL 2019

DECKHAND
DAYS

Midwest Edition
Copyright © 2019 by Tom Struve

First Printing: 2019

ISBN 9781726659734

BookworQs, LLC
Tom Struve
2935 N 148th Ave,
Goodyear AZ 85395

Copies of the authors books may be ordered at
https://bookworQs.com/

Special discounts may be available on quantity purchases by corporations, associations, educators, and others. For details, contact the author at the above listed address.

U.S. trade bookstores and wholesalers,
please contact the author Tom Struve
Tom.struve.17@gmail.com

A huge thank you
once again
to our editor
Julie
@ Free Range Editorial
http://www.freerangeeditorial.com/

I continue to be grateful
to all who are so willing
to share their awesome
towboat photos.

Especially Richard E. (Dick) Dunbar,
owner of Dick's Towboat Gallery.
http://www.towboatgallery.com/

And
Kyle Pfenning,
Veteran River Captain,
Hundreds of Awesome towboat videos at
https://www.youtube.com/user/marktwained.com

Dedication

This book is dedicated to
Captain Lowell Bailey

I owe you so much, Captain Lowell Bailey.
You were so good to me those many years ago.
I will always be incredibly grateful.

I am thrilled to dedicate this book to you,
your family,
and your legendary lifetime
as a river professional.

I raise a glass to you, Lowell.
**"Fair winds and
following seas, always,
to
YOU!"**

Introduction

"Sure, I can get you a job on the river. Yes, I can!"   *"Re-ally!?"*   *"You bet!" Captain Lowell Bailey continued. "I will take you down there myself and get you signed up."*

It was a great late-summer evening with the usual characters sitting around down at Captain Dick's Boat Dock. Captain Dick Schickling and his first mate (wife) De-De were putting things away before closing the small but successful marina for the day. Captain Bailey was a regular visitor, and he'd suggested more than once that he could get me a job on a towboat. Something was different this time, though.

"Really?" I asked again. "If I can count on that, I'll make plans to go to work on the boats next spring right after I graduate from high school."

So, that was how it all started. As he promised, Captain Bailey took me to the National Maritime Union Hall in Joliet, Illinois, a few months before I graduated. And, as planned (and dreamed about for my entire adolescence), I hired on with one of the major national towboat companies a few weeks after graduation.

This book focuses on those early years. These are stories of growing up along the river and then going to work as part of the deck crew on towboats. Join me for this journey, and you will see, hear, smell, and feel the river life as if you were there. I'll share tales of some wild, honest-to-goodness events along with my reflections, tempered by time and maturity. Each page includes footnotes explaining riverman terminology to help you out. Just look for the words in ***boldface***. The final chapter provides a glimpse into the third book in this series call PILOTHOUSE DAYS. Be sure to get your copy soon!

Our continued thanks to the many wonderful retail partners who offer our books to the public. We are VERY GRATEFUL!

Locks and Dams on Mississippi and Illinois Rivers.

Table of Contents-

Chapter 1
He's a Good Help!

"There he is!" roared Captain Dick as I came through the screen door. "I was hoping you would come by today, Moose! Got some work for you if you are willing."

"Sure," I said, always happy to be part of the action down on the riverfront in Prescott, Wisconsin, where I grew up.

Captain Dick's Boat Docks was a shack-like structure on the St. Croix River built on a large platform floating on empty fifty-five-gallon barrels. He needed a strong swimmer to move an almost fully flooded barrel underneath the longitudinal beams of the platform to replace a barrel that had sprung a leak. The old barrel had likely settled to the river bottom somewhere downstream and begun a new life as a shelter harboring a colony of fish just trying to survive another day.

"'Member how I showed ya how to do this?"

I nodded as Captain Dick grabbed hold of the homemade contraption he used to maneuver the heavy barrels. This tool cradled these large, very buoyant barrels and forced them into the water and under the dock. He pushed forward and down on the long tubes that served as levers. The barrel slowly lumbered its way into place just under the front edge of the dock.

I stripped off my t-shirt and tired sandals and sat on the edge of the platform. I slipped off the wooden dock into the cool St. Croix River. No life jacket; it would be a hindrance. I stayed close to the face of the dock countering the passing current by occasionally holding on to the wooden beams just above the water.

Mustering up considerable determination and a little courage, I began to muscle the barrel back and forth in the dark, heading for what I figured was the center of the platform. Darting around one obstacle after another, often holding my breath and submerging to push or pull, I welcomed each breath of air when I surfaced between the voids, being careful not to bang my head on the moldy boards of the deck just above.

Once I was in position, Captain Dick reminded me what to do next. "Make sure the barrel is turned so the large screw cap is up out of the water," he said, looking down at me from the edge of the platform closest to the channel of the river. "Then I'm gonna give you the end of this garden hose, and you gotta swim back under and insert it into that opening in the barrel that is above the water. You need to stay with it and keep it sucking all the water out of that barrel. When you're done you need to screw that cap back on tight!"

"Got it!"

"Are you holding up OK, Moose?" I noticed a look of concern on his tan, weathered face.

"I'm fine." I was more than fine. I was filled with pride about being trusted with adult-type work. I was very mature but still young at nine years old.

Soon the metal barrel was empty of river water, with the cap screwed on, holding that marvelous platform high and dry above the river. There were fifty or so barrels under there, all of them once used to transport oil. This was true recycling. Repurposing, long before anyone had ever heard that phrase!

View of the Captain Dicks Boat Docks today
and bridges where the St. Croix River
enters the Mississippi River at Prescott, WI.

When I climbed out of the water, I was pleased to see there was no longer a sag in the floor of the gas dock, mini-marina, and provisions store that was Captain Dick's pride and joy.

The maneuver I'd performed was actually a very risky procedure. Not sure anyone would consider doing it that way today. But Captain Dick had gone under with me to show me how it was done, so it never occurred to me it was anything but a chore that needed doing.

"Great job, Moose!" Next came the exuberant and excessively robust clap on the back and the loving, fatherly smile. Then with those long strides of his, he took off to tackle the next task of the day.

I'd been hanging around the river for a while when Captain Dick took a shine to me. He had tagged me with the nickname "Moose" early on and started finding small jobs I could help with. The most common reward for this work was his most earnest respect, gracious gratitude, and most likely a couple bottles of pop and maybe a candy bar. But, much, much more important, I felt like one of the crew. Welcome there anytime, part of the fabric of the place.

There was another serious perk. Whenever I asked if I could take out one of his small, twelve-foot homebuilt plywood rental rowboats, he said, "Sure. Just be careful. And you need to take a cushion."

A boat cushion/floatation device was all folks used in those days, back before the government ramped up regulations to protect us from ourselves.

I recall countless hours of the most blissful pleasure, at first just maneuvering those very practical small rowboats, eventually exploring every inlet and mystery spot along the Prescott riverfront. It was an idyllic aquatic playground for a young boy with Tom Sawyer-like yearnings.

Captain Dick's Boat Docks, now named Leo's Landing.
Same location as fifty-eight years ago.

Captain Dick's was the most welcoming of the marina stops along the riverfront in my hometown. There have been few occasions in my life that have brought me as much pleasure and pride as when I over-heard Captain Dick tell someone that I "was always a good help."

Captain Dick was a tall, skinny man with an easy, attractive smile and a touch of a Southern accent. His "first mate," DeeDee, was a lot slower to warm up, but after a time we became close. The couple had no children. Might have been why they showed me more than average kindness. The two made an awesome tag team.

Dick arrived at dawn every summer day to get the first of the fishermen and boaters rigged up and on their way. On weekdays, DeeDee would come by early to midafternoon, and Dick would head off to their house on the shore nearby for lunch and maybe a quick nap. Then they would switch places again until evening, when she generally came by again and they closed the place together.

Upbound towboat on the Mississippi at Mile Point 811.5 at the junction with the St. Croix River along the waterfront at Prescott, WI.

Weekends, it was all hands on deck. Pleasure boats came one after another to get gas and provisions, making for frenzied activity throughout the day.

It wasn't long before I was helping with one task or another almost daily in the summers. I felt so at home on the water and around folks boating and enjoying the river. Everyone who visited had a story to share or sat a bit to hear someone else's story during the less busy times.

A lot of these people were regulars. Mostly folks with holes in their daily calendars, which made a stop-in at Captain Dick's a pleasurable diversion.

People like Russ, "a vertically impaired man," at only three feet tall. In those days he was called a midget and was not offended. He had a sizable, successful farm outside of Hastings, Minnesota, just west of Prescott.

The railroad bridge tender was named Lyle Kidd. He sported greasy bib overalls and a railroad man cap, and always had dirty leather gloves sticking out of his left-hand pocket. I couldn't get enough of him. Anytime there was a lull in the conversation he could be counted on for a story about building or repairing the rails over his forty-five-year career.

Similarly, Francis Murphy, the highway bridge tender, seemed to always be around. The bridge tenders were paid to be available to open the bridges across the St. Croix just upstream from Captain Dick's. That only happened occasionally, but they needed to be around when required. Francis was the local gossip expert. There was very little in the small town of Prescott that escaped his notice. He did not generate chinwag, but he was an encyclopedia of current events and provided details whenever asked. His workmate, Frankie Huppert, was also a constant at Captain Dick's. He was a big, stocky guy. Almost as wide as he was tall. He didn't say a lot but had an attentive, friendly smile and a glorious laugh.

Other local river professionals would stop by frequently. Fellow captains or deck crew. Captain Dick and his peers entertained us all with Mark Twain-like anecdotes. Each was better that the last. I relished the stories they shared and never tired of visiting with them.

As a young boy, the author spent time with the highway bridgetenders
visiting the small building shown here at far left
on the upstream side of the historic US Highway 10 Bridge
across the St. Croix river at Prescott, Wisconsin.

The boaters and others who frequented the place were generously friendly and loved the atmosphere and Dick's demeanor, his always genial smile and friendly customer service. We were like characters in a continually changing play featuring a family that was very tenderly, but loosely, bound together. Always welcoming and loving and unassuming and better together than we were on our own. We shared a love of being on the water, on the river, in particular. Watching the current and the boats going by, an ever-changing canvas, with endless talented actors coming and going, each lending some wisdom, curiosity, or tone to the painting that was created anew at the start of each day.

Here, my earnest and very profound love for the river was an almost soulful affair. I was, going forward and for all time, certain to become a riverman.

Photo of deckhand coiling lock line on head deck of towboat.

"What is the earliest you can remember knowing you wanted to work on the river?"

"Jeez. I think I always did. When we first moved to town off the farm. I would hang around down by the river every day."

Chapter 2
My First Boat

"Hello, Moose!"

"G'morning, Dick!"

Grabbing the plastic dipper from its spot on the shelf, I headed out to bail the rainwater from the fishing boats. The walkway connecting the boat dock to the shore leaned a little this way and that as I strode the thirty or so feet back to the sandy shoreline. I started with the first of the six plywood boats closest to the railroad bridge.

It was early on a pristine summer morning. A little steamy, but the crystal-clear blue sky promised an enjoyable day. I loved this time of day down along the docks, and I felt blessed growing up in a sleepy small town of 1,500, with its modest Midwest demeanor.

In its earlier days, Prescott's Main Street hosted businesses, banks, and bars that primarily served farmers from the surrounding area. As the nearby twin cities of St. Paul and Minneapolis across the river in Minnesota elbowed to the east, Prescott had become more of a bedroom community with a country attitude. Everyone knew everyone else, and life moved along without much fanfare.

The St. Croix River enters the "muddy Mississippi" at Prescott, Wisconsin.

Life down along the banks of the river had the same small-town, no-fanfare flavor. The almost nonexistent midsummer St. Croix current was even less energetic just downriver from the railroad bridge. Only a few hundred feet downstream, the clear St. Croix River water mixed with the muddy Mississippi. The morning sun was still behind the tall century-old cottonwoods that line the rugged limestone riverbank there. I leaned down and dipped the rainwater from the bottom lowest corner of one boat then moved on to the next. I was just about to walk back along the rickety makeshift ramp connecting Dick's boat dock setup with the sandy shore to return the dipper, when I glanced up to see Captain Dick looking over the boats I'd just bailed out.

"You know, Moose, why don't I just give you one of these?"

The homebuilt wooden boat pictured here is very much like the author's first boat.

"Really!? Are you serious?"

Maybe Dick was sick of me always asking if I could take one out for an hour or two. Perhaps he was just being extraordinarily generous. Either way, you could not have found a happier nine-year-old within a hundred miles.

"Yeah, I'm gonna build some more this winter in my shop, and a couple of these are getting pretty ratty. You can have either of these two here. You've been really good about helping me out with things, and I'm grateful."

"Well, I don't know what to say except thanks!"

I spent some time carefully comparing the two boats. They were almost identical. Very simple plywood construction with essentially flat bottoms and three wooden seats. The boat I settled on was about twelve feet long, a foot longer than the other and with a slightly more pointed bow.

I laid my new prize up on her side to give her a good cleaning. I borrowed a bucket from the very basic collection of tools Captain Dick kept in the little cubby on the dock and spent the next thirty minutes rinsing the river sand, remnants of fishing bait, and trash from her bottom. Taking some of the tip money I'd earned tending and docking boats the past weekend, I headed up to Mercord's Hardware Store.

Historic downtown Main Street similar to
Prescott, WI, where Mercord's Hardware Store was located.

"Whaddaya need, Tommy?"

Dick Mercord was a burly, wide-framed character, forever present at the great historical-landmark store, one of the most robust and active destinations on the two blocks of Main Street.

"I need some of that half-inch yellow plastic rope to make lines and an anchor rope for my boat."

"Right this way."

Dick passed his brother Ron moving down the narrow aisles lined with endless hardware products. This old-fashioned mercantile offered everything. Paint, nuts, bolts, nails, cookware, you name it. In those days, televisions had glowing glass transformer-type tubes in the cabinet behind the large oval picture tube. If the TV quit working, you opened the back of the cabinet and removed whatever tube was not glowing. You brought the tube to the hardware store, and Dick or Ron would sell you a replacement. Problem solved.

Back in that other world, they had rows and rows of account books for charge accounts. Primarily used for farmers back then, I had my own charge account there too.

"How you doing today, Tommy?"

"I couldn't be better, Ron. How 'bout you?"

Ron didn't respond, intent as he was on fulfilling someone else's urgent request for some specific widget or bolt or fastener. Dick and I measured off fifty feet of that bright yellow rope, then Dick gave me my change, already deep into the next conversation helping another customer locate some obscure item that was always in stock at hardware stores back in the day.

The fine new yellow rope was stiff but sure to be tough, and I was happy as I made up some ten-foot lines for my little boat. I had found an old railroad brake shoe along the Burlington Northern railroad tracks and used it to make up a nice anchor with another thirty or forty feet of the yellow line. I visited my secret hiding place under the railroad bridge pier and dug out the two oars I had found floating along the shore in the spring floods. One was a little longer than the other, and each was an unusual color, but I didn't care. I was all set!

I pushed her back from shore and stepped aboard, almost breathless with excitement.

"You gotta have a cushion, ya know!" the old captain yelled from the dock.

I can't believe I forgot! I knew better than to head off without my boat cushion/flotation device. I raced up the rocky bank to my hiding spot and grabbed the old, torn-but-serviceable faded-red cushion that I'd stored with the rest of my treasures hoping for a day such as this.

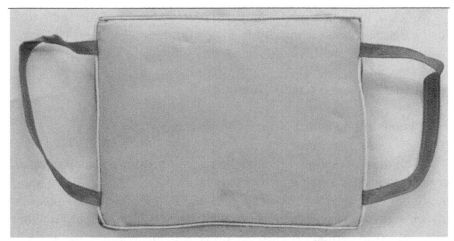
Boat cushions served double duty years ago as life preservers.

I tossed the cushion in the boat, then I shoved her slowly away from shore and climbed aboard. The oars were squeaking a little, so I took my bailing can and poured a small amount of St. Croix River water on and around each rusty steel oarlock. That took care of it.

Slowly rowing out from behind Captain Dick's, I crossed into the narrow St. Croix channel, moving toward the bridges. The bridge piers were protected from accidental barge rammings by a twenty-foot-high structure called a "sheer fence." It consisted of a series of long wooden pilings anchored/driven into the river bottom every few feet in a parallel line along the east, downstream side of the channel. Ten-inch-thick planks were fastened along the pilings, creating a solid wall. The pitch-black pilings and timber surfaces had the pungent odor of creosote. A popular preservative at the time, the chemical soup that was soaked into those construction timbers and pilings would later be determined to be extremely toxic and environmentally unsound. Up close in the summer heat, the odor was overwhelming.

I was enormously happy. I had never owned a boat but had dreamed endlessly of the freedom on the water that I was now experiencing. Maybe it was the idea of being in charge. I rowed for a long time upstream from the highway bridge.

It seemed so surreal to be in my own boat, spending time on the river without a care in the world. *Heaven.* Over that and the next few summers I explored every nook and cranny of the three marinas along our small town's shoreline in my little plywood boat.

One day, my dad brought home a tiny outboard motor.

"It's yours if you want it. Don't know if it runs. Had it down at the marina."

Elto ½-horsepower outboard motor just like the author's.

My dad worked for Prescott Marine at that time, the largest and most modern of the three marinas in Prescott. I couldn't wait to show the motor to Captain Dick. I knew I could count on him to help me get it running.

"Holy cow! Where'd ya git that? I had one of these a long time ago!"

"My dad said it was just layin' around down at the marina, and I could have it if I wanted. I knew that if anybody could help me get it going, it would be you."

He lifted the motor and lowered it into the tank he'd made to test outboard motors. He clamped it to the board that acted as a boat transom, then he filled the one-quart fuel tank.

Leos Landing, (formerly Captain Dicks Boatworks)
at the junction of the St. Croix and Mississippi Rivers.

"You're gonna need mixed gas, ya know. Forty to one. I'll fix you up with this little gas can I got."

I nodded.

"See here? This little float needle? You just push it up and down till a few drops of gas come out, then give 'er a pull."

He showed me how to operate the mechanism that controlled the throttle by sliding it sideways. I wound the piece of cord we'd used to make the starter rope around the grooved area atop the flywheel. One pull, and away it went! Smoky at first, but she ran like a dream!

We started and stopped it a couple more times there in the test tank, and then it was time to carry it out to my boat. It was extremely light, which made me wonder what kind of thrust it would generate. I pushed the boat away from the shore so there was enough water under the stern to keep the propeller from striking the bottom. I slid the clamp-like aluminum mounting sleeve down onto the boat's transom and turned the crank that would fasten it securely to the boat. I could hardly breathe. You'd think I was launching an aircraft carrier!

There were no decals or identifying marks on my motor by the time it got to me. It was only decades later I learned it was a 1/2-horsepower 1937 Evinrude Elto Pal. All I knew then, and all I needed to know, was I was at the helm of my first boat with an actual outboard motor.

I was ecstatic! Hours and days, months and years of boating pleasure followed. With only 1/2 horsepower we didn't go far, but I loved every luxurious minute on board my own boat.

The author in his small boat would face the wind and waves traveling downstream out of Lake St. Croix, here right under this historic US Highway 10 bridge in Prescott.

Among my fondest memories of my youth are the days the north or northwest wind blew straight down the St. Croix River upstream from the highway bridge. I would take my little boat out, point her into that wind, and steer her directly into the two- to three-foot rollers that cascaded down the river. The motor was too weak to provide any headway on days with strong winds, so we just cut through one wave after another, not really going anywhere. I would just ride that frisky water, facing into the wind and the occasional splash of water, grinning like a fool.

There was nowhere I'd rather be than the river. I'd found my place in the world.

Downbound towboat on Mississippi River.

"You began looking after yourself early in life. Tell me about that."

"Didn't think much about that. Loved all the things I did at that time. Lots of great learning about life. Once my mom died, I had to take care of myself."

Chapter 3
Lime Juice

"Lime juice. D'you git it?"

"I thought you got it!"

Big, roaring, raucous laughs as Big John and his merry crew began loading coolers. It was Sunday afternoon in early July down at the Price Rite Liquor courtesy dock along the riverfront in Prescott. I served as the unofficial but generally recognized dock boy there, right upstream from Captain Dick's, and it was a wonderful way to spend summer days.

A shirttail cousin had stayed with us for a couple weeks the summer before. He lived on the coast in California and introduced my brother and me to the concept of hanging around where boaters dock and tending to their needs for tips.

My older brother spent his summer days at the Steamboat Inn dock just north of the highway bridge, and I watched over the boaters at the Price Rite courtesy dock just downstream in Prescott.

Steamboat Inn and dock on the St. Croix looking east
from across the river at Point Douglas Beach.

"Tommy, you sure you don't want a beer?"

More laughter followed as the others marveled at how bold and reckless Big John was when he was drink-boating. That was what it was called back then. Long before today's almost zealous aversion to drinking and driving, it was not unusual to drink to excess while boating.

John, his buxom and ultra-friendly wife, and two or three other boatloads of comrades arrived every Sunday around lunchtime like clockwork. They would laugh uproariously, sharing stories about near accidents and other adventures along the journey downstream from St. Paul through Lock 2 in Hastings to the Price Rite courtesy dock to restock for the trip back.

"Thanks, Big John, but no. I can't do that. I would git in trouble," I said, smiling. Like most ten-year-olds, my list of favorite beverages didn't include beer.

Big John and his people were always extremely nice to me. As the dock boy, I would catch and secure their mooring lines when they approached the dock, prevent serious crashes, assist people on and off the boats, and watch to make sure no one messed with any of their things while they were upstairs in the liquor store. Just like I did for everyone who stopped by.

Minnesota Sunday liquor sales were limited to restaurants, so the Price Rite Liquor Store did a land-office business on Sundays as they were just across the state line. The owners at that time were very professional and treated all their customers like family. Regulars were frequently greeted by name, and it was not uncommon for buyers to receive deep discounts, especially if they bought in bulk.

Mr. Carlson and Mr. Simonez were at the top of Prescott's social elite, and their prosperous and lively liquor business made them among the wealthiest in our tiny town.

Big John's twenty-foot fiberglass boat was styled like a cabin cruiser but much smaller. There was a forward cabin equipped with a modest galley and bathroom. The rear half of the boat featured an elevated deck with associated furniture and two captain's chairs that allowed an elevated perch behind a generous windshield. A portable bimini top was almost always down, and John and his shapely bride had the darkest tans I'd ever seen.

I remember that Big John's boat had a 90-horsepower Mercury, which was the biggest outboard motor (literally and figuratively) that you could buy in 1962.

Like Big John's boat — circa 1960.

Outboards were polluting, smoky, unreliable, and loud affairs at that time, and left a generous film of oil on the surface of the surrounding water.

"Tommy, how old are you?" asked Big John's wife.

"I just turned ten. Always been big for my age," I responded. Almost everyone commented about that. I guess a six-foot-tall ten-year-old was something of a curiosity.

"You sure are a nice boy. Here. This is for you. Thanks fer takin' such nice care of us."

She handed me a few folded bills, then hugged me, pressing me in close and lingering longer than I was comfortable with. She did that a lot. But I couldn't complain too much. I knew I'd have a tip of anywhere from three to five dollars from her. In the early 60's, five dollars was *a lot* of money.

John's gang would then fire up their smoky outboards, and I would cast off their mooring lines and send them on their way with a robust farewell.

Occasionally boaters would go up the concrete stairs and continue across the street to one of the three modest but rollicking bars along the two city blocks of Prescott's Main Street. Some returned after only a short time, and some enjoyed hours of revelry before returning. On weekends I kept watch over their boats late into the night, and most of the time the tips reflected that, so it was well worth my while.

My mother would bring me an evening meal when she could. She was a nurse and worked lots of extra hours. She was okay with me working on the dock as long as she knew where I was. It was a different time, and youngsters were allowed generous latitude in decisions that impacted how much fun we had.

Every now and then some kids from Hastings would make the five-mile walk to Prescott along the railroad tracks. Sometimes they would bully me and give me a general, all-around hard time. Once, one of them threw a lit M-80 firework down at me as I was tending boats on the dock. It bounced up off the dock and exploded one inch behind my left calf just below my knee. It caused a serious burn, and I have a scar on my leg and profound hearing loss as a result.

I was hesitant to squeal on the Hastings boys, sure it would only cause the bullying to escalate. I did go visit with Captain Dick though, and I told him all about it. He was furious.

"You come and git me next time those little bastards show up."

"Are you sure?"

"Yes. You jist come down here and git me, and I'll make the little shits stay away from you."

A few weeks later, they were once again at the top of the steps around the old wooden picnic table. The jeering began, and Captain Dick must have overheard. Before I knew it, he had come over and walked up to the boys without their noticing.

Prescott's riverfront showing the courtesy dock between the highway and the railroad bridges.

Captain Dick grabbed one of the boys by the collar and backed him up to the picnic table and just slapped him silly. The boy cried like a baby and eventually wriggled out of his grip. He ran, stumbling along till he caught up with the others hightailing it back over the railroad bridge into Minnesota. Those boys never came back. One more reason Captain Dick was my hero.

My mother had a brain aneurism early the next spring and passed away. My father provided for the four of us kids, but we moved from very little adult supervision to none at all. But life goes on.

I continued enjoying my summer days down on the river. My older brother became a parking lot attendant at the Steamboat Inn, so I moved into his dock boy spot. It was a much larger courtesy dock, with a very robust weekend business, and as a result it was more financially rewarding.

On summer weekends I often arranged boats in rafts, one alongside the other, sometimes five to seven boats wide. I was constantly shifting them in and out with folks coming and going.

Holiday weekends were especially busy. Customers were more than grateful when I would make space for them to moor so they could go up the stairs for some high-end dining and drinking. The tips were generous, and I made lots more cash than I had at the Price Rite courtesy dock. I also learned a great deal about life there.

Now a sage twelve-year-old, I was beginning to understand a bit more about the adult world of romance. My observations, along with more frequent encounters with mature, sometimes overly familiar female customers helped speed me along from preadolescence to post-puberty.

I learned that very well-to-do people are almost always genuinely gracious, kind, generous, and happy. I learned that lots of business is conducted while entertaining clients. I looked after small boats and medium boats and the most luxurious giant yachts one can imagine. I was fascinated by the extravagant appointments of many of the larger yachts and stunned by the vastly different lifestyle of their owners.

"Hi, Tommy! Good to see you, son!"

Willard Munger, for whom a popular bike trail in northern Minnesota is named, was one of the regulars. Arriving most afternoons at the helm of a new-every-year forty-foot or larger Trojan cabin cruiser, he entertained clients almost every night of the week. His business was insurance.

"What are you gonna be, Tommy?"

"I hope you are saving all your tips to go to college, right?" his gracious wife would always ask.

The Steamboat Inn had a larger courtesy dock and a more upscale clientele than the Price Rite Liquor Store dock.

"Yes sir, Mr. and Mrs. Munger. I am glad to see you again today. Let me slide over our best and largest set of portable steps for you and your guests. Right away!"

On weekdays, boaters arrived mostly toward dinner time. On weekends, the Steamboat Inn was an all-day stop. I stayed well into the night seven days a week in the summer and on weekend nights in the fall after school started back up. Most times the customers acknowledged the care I provided for their boats and property and rewarded me handsomely. Many were regulars, and I enjoyed being recognized as their personal attendant.

Every few days thunderstorms changed the mundane into an adventure. The Steamboat dock was upstream from the highway bridge precisely where the St. Croix widened about one-half mile to the west towards Minnesota. I could see the lightning across and above the high Minnesota bank long before the storms arrived and could always smell the rain as it approached.

Occasionally, wall clouds slowly advanced, almost black on the distant horizon. I would tighten and add mooring lines to all the boats where I could, and once the storm struck I would hurry up the concrete steps and watch from the shelter of the awning.

A hand-sized transistor radio was my constant companion, and on many summer evenings the Minnesota Twins baseball broadcast helped me through long hours of waiting. That and the carp.

Between the rocks shown here and the shore is
where the giant carp would feed in evenings.

Between the dock and the nearby sheer limestone shoreline, schools of giant carp would nurse in the evenings. Sucking at the surface with almost human-sized lips, they consumed most everything that had floated into the still, eddy-free shoreline water. These twenty- to forty-pound prehistoric-looking monsters were easy to fool, and I

39

would sometimes buy a bag of stuffing mix at the local bakery. This was prior to Stove Top Stuffing, and bakeries recycled stale bread that didn't sell into dried cubes that made excellent stuffing for poultry. Sprinkled liberally and floating on the water, one of the crust pieces would have a giant hook in it connected to forty-pound-test fishing line. Quite the battle would ensue once that piece of crust with the hook disappeared from the surface. I always let them go, mostly because I didn't know what to do with a fish that big!

Giant carp feeding at the surface behind the Steamboat Inn dock.

I will never forget all those smells. River water, approaching rain, two-stroke outboard motor exhaust, and gasoline and trash floating on the water. The smell of beer and liquor drifting on the breeze from the decks of those well-appointed boats. The aroma of the excellent cuisine served by the restaurant.

Hypnotic and memorable and inviting. Those days of learning from people's behavior, practicing how to be charming, and the very earliest years of learning about working to make ends meet.

All of that and being on the water loving every minute of it. What a marvelous youth!

"How did you get your first towboat job?"

"I was so fortunate. A captain named Lowell Bailey took me under his wing. He lived in Prescott and was one of the captains of the MV *Sioux* there. He took me down to Joliet, Illinois, and got me signed up at the National Maritime Union Hall."

Chapter 4
Boat Docks to My First Towboat

"I will git you a job on the river, Tom. Yes, I will!"

The summer before my senior year of high school, one of the frequent visitors to Captain Dick's was a guy named Captain Lowell Bailey. He was one of two captains at that time working aboard the MV *Sioux*, a splendid towboat moored at Prescott. (MV is the abbreviation for Motor Vessel.) The MV *Sioux* made weekday trips up the St. Croix River to the Northern States Power coal-fired King Power Plant just downstream from Stillwater, Minnesota.

The towboat MV *Sioux* upbound on the St. Croix River
in front of Prescott, Wisconsin.

Captain Bailey and Captain Dick talked endlessly about the river and their experiences, and I was enraptured with it all. Captain Bailey was very gregarious and more than once he'd said to me, "I will git you a job on the river, Tom." We didn't really get into the details at first, but those words seemed to me to be all my dreams coming true.

The next year, Captain Bailey moved to Prescott after becoming the port captain for Twin City Barge and Towing Company. Twin City Barge was a modest towboat, fleeting, and barge repair company in St. Paul, very nearby. Captain Bailey was now always around town, and every time I saw him he reminded me that he would help me get a job on the river that coming spring.

Captain Bailey was *very* well-known for being a big talker. He often told rollicking and outrageous stories, loved a few cocktails, and was always the center of attention, creating loud and raucous fun times wherever he went. Some years later I learned that my dad had had a stern discussion with Captain Bailey a few months before I was due to graduate. The conversation concerned the fact that his son (of whom he was very fond) was counting on Captain Bailey to help him get a job on the river.

Captain Bailey did follow through on his promise. He arranged for me to accompany him down to the Lemont, Illinois, offices of Twin City Barge. I will never forget how it felt to arrive in that industrial canal area right outside of Chicago. Earlier, simply driving through Chicago on the freeway for the first time was a big enough thrill. All the oversized billboards and lights. It all was pretty breathtaking for a young man who had not traveled a great deal.

We drove slowly down the gravel entrance road to the Twin City Barge offices along the canal. The February weather included a little snow, and it was cold when we arrived. We climbed on to the towboat MV *Pawnee*, which was tied off against the limestone concrete wall next to the offices.

"Hello, partner!" shouted a loud voice. "How are you doin', you big, cross-eyed bugger, you?" It was Captain Jack Moore who was port captain for Twin City Barge in the Chicago area. Lots of clapping on the back and handshakes and laughing and more laughing.

Captain Bailey introduced me. "Jack, this here is Tom Struve. He's a buddy of mine that I met when I was runnin' the *Sioux* in Prescott." He continued, "I brought him down with me to get him registered at the union hall, so he can get right out when he comes back down later in the spring."

Jack said, "Sounds like a plan, man! Let's git you two set up with some rooms, and then we'll head up to Tom's Place for dinner."

I was on board a real live towboat! It was exhilarating! The smells were overwhelming. The familiar musty aroma of river was more overpowering here than I'd ever experienced. In addition, there were strong odors of diesel fuel, motor oil, and machinery. I followed behind as they led me to one of the deck rooms normally used by deckhands on board the towboat. They gave me a set of sheets and a blanket and showed me how to operate the heater. Captains Bailey and Moore went forward to make up their beds in the captain's area of the towboat, and we met up on deck a few minutes later.

43

"Whiskey for me, and fresh horses for my men," Captain Bailey shouted above the din as we walked into Tom's Place in downtown Lemont. Captain Moore roared with laughter. The bartender, after whom the tiny gin mill is named, greeted all three of us with a broad smile and firm handshakes.

Historic Blatz Beer sign announcing, "Tom's Place" in Lemont, Illinois. The same façade and sign today as greeted us that February night in 1970.

"Good to see you boys! What'll ya have?"

"Tap beers and a bump for all," Captain Bailey said.

And so, a memorable evening began. Over the coming years, I would find myself many times at Tom's Place in Lemont, sharing river yarns and laughs with fellow towboaters. The stories and camaraderie of that special night will always be with me. I was sure I'd died and gone to heaven!

The next day dawned crisp, with a clear blue sky. Captain Moore and Captain Bailey met with business managers for a couple of hours in the morning. I went for a walk and continued to take in all the sights and smells of this marine industrial location.

A vast dry dock facility operated nearby, and various towboats and barges were high and dry propped up on marine ways. (Marine ways are horizontal supports under vessels on shore so they can be welded and repaired on all sides.)

Upper Illinois River at Lemont, Illinois. Narrow channel and always bustling!

I was like a kid in a candy shop. I didn't know where to look first: the flash of welders arcing and loaders and cranes moving about in a frenzy; the dozens of barges of all kinds moored together like a jigsaw puzzle and tied to the limestone walls of the fleeting areas; towboats moving here and there. It was like a dream come true.

Following the now familiar backslapping and handshaking, Captain Bailey and I said goodbye and traveled the twenty or so miles over to Joliet. We parked across from the small local office of the National Maritime Union. Joliet is a historic old town, and the neighborhood where the union hall was located had seen better days. A large blue sign at the opposite end of the one-story building indicated that the steel workers union office was there too.

Captain Bailey introduced himself and me to George, the union representative. George was a small gentleman who seemed even more diminutive alongside Marie, his second in command. Marie was a robust gal with more makeup and jewelry than I had ever seen before. I am sure I must have gawked; it was all very surreal. I filled out a form, paid my registration fee, and we went on our way.

Captain Bailey took me around the corner and down two blocks. He pointed out the multistory YMCA there, which provided simple, inexpensive rooms to the public. Captain Bailey suggested that might be a good safe place to start out when I returned.

On the way back north we traveled through Wisconsin heading back to Prescott. Captain Bailey explained that it was a good strategic move to get me registered so far ahead of time. It had to be done in person, and at that location. When I returned to the hiring hall for a riverboat deckhand job that spring after graduation, my registered union card would be the most senior among the inexperienced union members in the office, a big advantage. I would then be entitled to the first deckhand job that was not taken by experienced union members waiting for jobs at the union hall.

The strategy played out exactly as planned, and while I did spend ten days waiting for that first job, the wait was completely forgotten when I finally shipped out of the hall that very first time.

The jobs that came into the union hall were posted four times a day, twice in the morning and twice again in the afternoon. Some days no jobs came into the hall. The newbies like me were assigned "D-card" status, and only after any available jobs were turned down by experienced, active union members at the hall could any of us with a D-card take that newly posted job.

Author's first towboat assignment, MV *Albert E. Heekin*.

The moment finally came, and I was assigned my first river deckhand job, aboard the MV *Albert E. Heekin*. The *Albert E. Heekin* was a nasty, old, grungy live-aboard harbor towboat. Eight hundred horsepower and 144 feet long, it pushed eight barge tows of coal upstream from Joliet to the many power plants in Chicago.

It wasn't a very desirable posting I soon found out, but it got me that first job, and my union status from that point on was "experienced." The moment you stepped aboard your first towboat to work you moved from a D-card to a B-card. B-card status turned waiting for a deck job in the union hall from a long, exasperating sojourn to, in most cases, a day or two wait.

MV *Dresden*.
Authors second deckhand assignment.
An Illinois River Valley Line coal towboat.

Once I was a full-fledged professional riverman, I worked aboard many kinds of boats, eager to find the right fit. At first, I worked frequently on Illinois River coal line-haul towboats. I also worked on small, live-aboard harbor boats for a company called Material Service that mostly moved sand and aggregates into and around Chicago.

I felt especially blessed the day I shipped out onto an assignment on my first Upper Mississippi line-haul towboat. This happened about six months into my river career. The boat was the MV *WS Rhea*, towing barges for the Valley Line Company.

MV *WS Rhea*, legendary class "big" towboat
Author's first line-haul towboat
sailing past his hometown of Prescott, Wisconsin
on the Mississippi River.

In those years, the Valley Line Company was one of a handful of premier barge line companies, and an assignment on any of their live-aboard line-haul boats was prestigious and coveted. My dream of traveling past my hometown of Prescott, Wisconsin, as part of a towboat crew was finally a reality.

"How long did you have to spend at the union hall in Joliet before you got your first assignment?"

"It was Thursday of the second full week when I got my first towboat. I was spending about $6 per day including my room at the YMCA and one or two meals at the local burger joint. I was just about out of money."

Chapter 5
Welcome Aboard?

"**G**et your stuff stowed and get your work clothes on! You're on watch!"

Wow. A rather gruff welcome to my first towboat job, aboard the MV *Albert E. Heekin*. It was just after one o'clock on an early June afternoon, and I was getting on board at the wharf barge for the Valley Line Company in Joliet. We were in a wide part of the Illinois River, with dozens of barges moored on both sides, immediately upstream from the Brandon Road Lock. The long bridge for Interstate 80 crossed high overhead.

I had no idea where to "stow my stuff." There were no signs saying: Deckhand Crew Quarters This Way. A square-jawed, sweaty older gentleman with tattered, oily clothes and an unkempt beard was making his way forward in the same passageway I was going into. I stuck out my hand, hoping it was appropriate to introduce myself.

"Hi. I'm Tom. Looking for my room."

"You the *relief* for that guy that just got off?"

"Guess so. Just getting on board now."

"Follow me, I'll show ya down there. I'm Gary, the chief engineer."

He did a one-eighty and went back the way he had come. I followed him down the noisy hall. A handrail was unevenly fastened to the wall, which was covered in bright white high-gloss paint with greasy stains all along the dimly lit hallway. We went down three or four steps to a T intersection then turned left. He opened a cabin door and found it dark, the shape of someone asleep under a sheet on the bottom of the bunk beds. We went back the direction we'd come, past the steps to another cabin door. That room was unoccupied. The lights were on and the linens gone from the top bunk. A couple of chairs sat in opposite corners, and there was a tiny sink below a cracked, stained mirror. It was hot in there. Noisy. Smelled like fuel and oil and mold and the river.

So, this was it. My new life. Not exactly as romantic as I had envisioned, but there I was. I thanked Gary and set my stuff in the least occupied corner of the small room. I took a moment to slide the rusty metal folding chair over and stood on it so I could see out the window. Holy cow. I was looking out almost at the level of the river outside. The room was primarily below the waterline, and because of that, the ceiling was markedly high. Noisy. Smelly. Warmer than it seemed it should be.

relief – the replacement for a crew member who got off the boat

I checked the small air conditioner sticking out of the wall next to the sink. It was turned on high and had a pretty good chill coming out. Just having trouble keeping up.

I opened my trunk and got out my gloves and my steel toe work boots. George, the sharp-talking but kind union hall business agent had advised me to be sure I had those essentials when I boarded. "And get yourself some t-shirts!" I tied my boots, stuck the gloves in my back pocket, then headed up the steps and down the corridor.

The end of the corridor came out onto an elevated walkway that spanned the width of the towboat along the very forward portion of the engine room. Really noisy. Hurt-your-ears noisy. I understood why Gary had those headset hearing protectors around his neck. Two giant diesel motors. Very hot and very noisy. Lots of pipes and baffled muffler attachments, all painted a high-gloss yellow with various amounts of sooty staining.

Two enormous diesel engines shown in marine engine room.

"Come on! Git out here and help!" a gigantic man in dirty clothes encased in a dirtier, ill-fitting once-bright-orange life jacket yelled at me.

I stepped out on the side walkway (called the "guard" on a towboat) and watched this guy grab a heavy, greasy, thick cable and wrap it around the *timberhead* of the barge we had just pushed up against. I tried to help pull, and he mostly jerked the cable his way to indicate what seemed to be disdain for me.

"You're new, ain'tcha?"

"Yes, sir. My name is Tom. Yours is?"

"I'm Jim, and I'm sick of the revolving door that this damn boat is. I can't keep any good men on here. Just one after another of you green pukes! One of these days I'm gonna get off this damn old river…"

Old Jim really made me feel welcome. One good thing: I knew right from the get-go how this was going to go. Clearly this was an opportunity to make the best of it.

"It's true, Jim. I'm new. But I want you to know I will do whatever you tell me, and with a smile. I'm not afraid of work, and I have always been a quick learner."

"Yeah. We'll see about that. Grab that set of *toothpicks* and that *cheater bar* and come with me. Get a damn life jacket on!"

There were a few life jackets lying around, so I grabbed what looked like the cleanest and wrestled my arms through the holes and fastened the clips at my chest and waist. Toothpicks? Cheater what?

"Jim. Not sure what you mean by toothpicks and a cheater tar."

timberhead- vertical tubular mooring fittings. See photo on page fifty-three.
toothpicks - steel rods about one inch in diameter and two to three feet long used to keep the ends of the ratchet from turning when screwing together or tightening it
cheater bar - tubular pipe two to three inches in diameter that is placed over the ratchet handle to give the user extra leverage to tighten the ratchets

"Cheater *bar*, not *tar*, you damn fool! That steel pipe right there, about three feet long. And toothpicks are the steel rods in that pile right next to the pipes. You're gonna need two toothpicks and one cheater bar, and you just need to figger on having them with you all the time."

The deckhand shown here is using a cheater bar to unfasten rigging.

I picked the ***tools*** that seemed to be the least greasy and filthy and followed Jim across the front of the towboat and stepped across what I learned later was called the ***head log*** onto a barge. Jim had grabbed that big, greasy wire cable on the opposite front corner of the boat, and this time when I reached to help, he released his grip, and I suddenly had the full weight and pull of it. Determined not to react in any negative way, I could see Jim grinning, having just pulled his first work prank of the day, at my expense. Again, filed away immediately was the knowledge that I needed to be acutely aware of this dangerous work setting and to expect more than an occasional "testing."

tools - toothpicks and cheater bar (cheater pipe)
head log - front end of the towboat where it contacts the barge(s)

The captain operated the noisy *winch* motors, and the cables tightened to secure our boat to the barges we were picking up. Jim and I headed forward, walking between two loaded coal barges, the rear of a group of eight. The steel deck walkways along the edges of the barges were almost completely obscured by loose coal that fell there during unloading at the coal-fired power plants we were going to.

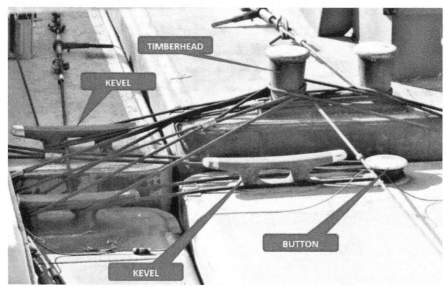

Fittings (kevels, buttons, and timberheads)
used to anchor rigging to fasten barges together to make a tow.

Stepping carefully, I maneuvered around lots of deck *fittings* called *kevels* and *buttons* and many timberheads, which were mostly on the corners. Jim seemed to pay no attention at all, and I sensed that over

winch - a towboat device that reels in or lets out flexible-steel cables used to fasten barges and/or towboats together and to one another. Winches can be manually operated or can be electric or hydraulic powered.

fittings - timberheads, kevels, buttons. These are devices built into the decks of towboats or barges used to fasten rigging or lines. See photo with details on page fifty-four.

kevel – also called a "cavel." Fitting built into the deck of a towboat or barge used to fasten lines or rigging to another fitting

button - a fitting welded to the deck of a barge or towboat most commonly used to anchor one end of a set of rigging

time, navigating the uneven footing became second nature out on the tow. We stopped where the two barges closest to the towboat were connected front and back, and Jim showed me what my work was to be. Lots of dirty, thick, greasy flexible- steel cables running every direction, hooked to threaded turnbuckles called *ratchets*.

"Ya put yer toothpicks in the ends of the ratchets so the ends don't turn. Then tighten 'em as far as you can by hand. When they git tight you stick the cheater bar on the end of the ratchet handle and crank some more. Like this."

He showed me how to insert the three-foot-long, one-inch-diameter steel rods—toothpicks—into the ends of the ratchet and how to determine which way to turn the ratchet barrel to tighten the heavy cables.

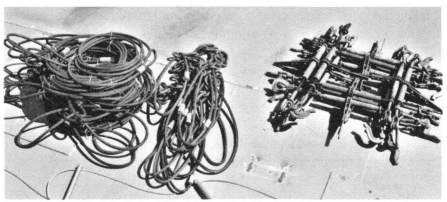

Rigging: Coiled up flexible-steel wires at left, chain straps in center, and ratchets stacked at right

"You're gonna stay here and continue to tighten all the rigging you see here. The very same thing that we just did repeated over and over. I'm gonna *turn us loose* so we can head on up the river."

ratchet - sometimes called a "turnbuckle." This is a tool with threaded ends that contract when the *ratchet barrel* (center) is turned. It is used to tighten the cables that fasten barges together.
turn us loose - untie the towboat and/or barges from mooring

"How tight do they need to be?" I asked.

"As tight as you can get 'em and then two more turns." Was that an attempt at humor? Seemed likely.

So, crank I did. I repeatedly inserted the toothpicks as shown and hand tightened each ratchet and then followed with the cheater pipe (another name for a cheater bar).

After a time, the horn honked from the top of the pilothouse behind me (more commonly known as a *whistle* on a towboat). I learned later that blast of the whistle told Jim to cast off the last lines. It was the signal that we were leaving the *mooring*.

I noted that Jim gave a big *two-hands-up-in-the-air gesture* (like a football ref signaling a touchdown) just after the whistle blew. That hand signal is towboat speak for *all gone* or all turned loose. It was my introduction to deck crew-to-pilothouse on-deck communication protocol.

I kept tightening each of the ratchets and was feeling rather full of myself, confident Jim would be super impressed when he returned from his more important chores. I had tightened each as far as it seemed like it was possible. I worried that if I kept up, I might break something. The wires and turnbuckles creak and groan when being tightened.

When Jim came back to where he had left me approximately twenty minutes before, he did the strangest thing. He picked up his cheater bar—it looked at least a foot longer than mine and had a sheen to it, a sign of constant use—and began to walk about the coupling I was so pleased with. Without warning or explanation, he swung his

whistle - most common name for a towboat horn. Most towboat horns today are air powered. Decades ago a towboat whistle was powered by steam.
mooring - commonly understood to be anywhere along shore where a vessel can be secured to some kevel or timberhead that is stationary
hands-up-in-the-air gesture - deck person indicating that the towboat or barges are turned loose. This indicates *all gone.*
all gone - towboat or barges are all turned loose

cheater pipe over his head and brought it down, slamming over and over onto the thick wires holding the barges together. And just like that, most of them were so loose I might as well not have done anything. I was perplexed and a bit embarrassed.

When he stopped pounding on the cables, he inserted his toothpicks and started in doing what I had just done, motioning to me to join him. What I didn't know was that the tightening and subsequent beating of the thick, taut wire is how it always goes. The wires need to be cajoled in this fashion to ensure that the contact with the timberheads and barge fittings has no movement at all. I was disappointed to see my hard work go for naught but learned quickly that this was how it is done.

"You can't get the rigging in the **steering coupling** too tight, ever! He started in again, slamming his cheater pipe down onto the spans between deck fittings. This time only one or two of the wires needed further attention. When he was satisfied, he motioned to me to stop pumping my cheater pipe back and forth on the ratchet. "Next coupling," he said as I followed him.

I felt some level of relief to know that there apparently was a tightness level that was good enough and allowed myself to cautiously glance sideways at the riverbank in downtown Joliet slowly going by.

Railroad bridge in raised position on Illinois River, downtown Joliet, Illinois.

steering coupling - the first fore and aft connection (*coupling*) of barges forward of the bow of the towboat. This coupling gets more stress than the others and must be extra sturdy and tight.

We were underway. *So this is how it is*, I thought. I was thrilled to be there, for the first time looking out toward shore from a working towboat instead of the other way around.

We arrived at the next coupling and repeated the tightening process. Jim tripped at one point. "Damn no good co*#s&cking river!"

He caught himself before falling, but one hand came down hard on the steel deck, and he shook his wrist, scowling and cussing again. I was impressed that he caught himself the way he did.

I noticed that he didn't wear any gloves. His huge callous-covered hands were almost coal black. I thought it best not to ask him about that, glancing at my brand-new gloves, already torn in three places and filthy after only an hour of this hard work.

"What the hell would cause a young guy like you to come to work out here on this damn old river? You got no better sense than that?"

"Always wanted to be out here. Grew up on the banks of the Mississippi in a tiny town in Wisconsin. Never wanted to do anything else."

"You get as many years as I do in, and you're gonna look back and wonder what the hell you were thinkin'!"

"Where you from, Jim?"

"Beardstown, Illinois. Seems like that whole goldang town works out here on the river. All anybody there ever knew. Got a brother and two uncles and one aunt that work on the boats."

"Is Beardstown downriver from here? Will we pass by?"

"Shit, no! This old piece of shit boat don't do nothin' but shuffle back and forth in and outta the city. Ten hours from now we drop this piece-of-shit tow, and then we pick up empty barges coming back south a couple at a time and then do the same daagone thing all over again.

It's like being caught in a dangblessed revolving door. One of these days I'm gonna quit this damn old stinking boat...."

One of several bascule-style bridges passed
while navigating along the Illinois River at downtown Joliet, Illinois.

By this time, we were beginning to pass through the series of **bascule bridges** that cross what seemed to be a very narrow section of river in Joliet.

I was fascinated by the many things I had never experienced before. The Mississippi and St. Croix Rivers where I grew up had sand and mud shores and lots of vegetation. This was all concrete and industrial buildings or apartments right at the edge of the river. Car after car hurried across the metal grates of the bridge decks making lots of noise. The captain blew a long signal on the boat's whistle and at what seemed like the last second, a bunch of red lights started flashing, and a bell clanged loudly. Crossing arms descended quickly on traffic and walking lanes on both sides of the bridge. The bridge raised up, splitting in the middle, gargantuan steel gears exposed on the shore bases as the towboat passed through where the bridge just was.

Jim and I were still tightening wires on the third, and final, coupling, the one farthest out from the towboat. We were pushing eight loaded coal barges, two barges wide and four barges long. It was much quieter there except for the noises of traffic and the surrounding city life.

bascule bridge - a bridge over a waterway that splits in the middle. Each side is raised from a pivot on shore, allowing river traffic to pass under. Bascule bridges typically open and close rapidly.

The diesel motors of the towboat were less deafening out there *on the tow*.

My mind wandered, and I felt a remarkable and overwhelming sense of gratitude for my good fortune. It was almost euphoric, the sense of belonging and well-being I found working on the water. I'd known, always, that it would be like that.

Jim's lazy Southern Illinois drawl once again brought me back to the present.

"We're comin' up on the lock in about an hour, so you have a little time to yourself once we git this couplin' done. I'm gonna check all the barges for leakers, and we'll most likely need to drag out a pump or two. Meantime, git your ass back to the boat and go to the can, git some water. Whatever you gotta do 'cause we'll be out on the tow the rest of the *watch* lockin' through."

"Gotcha," I said. "Thanks for letting me know."

What a great day, indeed.

on the tow - when crew members are out on the barges the towboat is transporting
watch - towboat workers on line-haul boats typically work two six-hour shifts for a total of twelve hours per workday. The forward watch is six a.m. to noon and six p.m. to midnight. The after watch is the opposite of that.   ***

rigging - the combination of flexible-steel cables, chain straps, links, and ratchets that are placed on a tow to hold it together as one unit
one set of rigging is commonly understood to be one ratchet, one wire, and one chain strap.
Three primary configurations for "laying" (installing) a set of rigging:
      1. *Fore and aft wire* - The wire is looped (usually three ways) around fittings ("kevels" as in picture on page fifty-four) on each barge and connected to the ratchet and deck fittings at the center of the barge. This connects the barge in the rear to the one in front of it.
      2. *Breast wire* - This can be any combination of wires, chain straps, and ratchets that holds the barges together side by side. This connects a barge to the one next to it.
      3. *Scissor wire* - Also called "jockey wires," these wires are laid diagonally on top of fore and aft rigging. Their primary purpose is to keep the entire tow of barges as stiff as can be (locked together as one tight unit). This keeps adjacent barges from moving back and forth alongside each other.

"What was your first impression of your first towboat? Were you excited, scared, disappointed?"

"I remember the smells and the noise and the enormity of it all. And the sense of this marvelous industrial setting and existence that is very exclusive. Everybody looks at towboats going by from the shore and wonders what it is like."

Chapter 6
Holy Cow. What's All This?

I stopped briefly back in my room for a quick examination, my highest priority, only slightly above exploring the remainder of the towboat. It was dark in there, and a fellow crew member was asleep in the lower bunk. It was even more claustrophobic in the dark. Glad that I'd opened the door slowly, I backed away out quietly. *So that's how it works. One guy occupies the room while the deckhand on the other watch is working.*

I really wanted to check out more about the room being below the waterline. That sure didn't strike me as very safe. I guessed it would have to wait.

I walked down the side deck along the length of the towboat, and as I passed the open engine room windows and doors, I spotted the ear-muffed chief engineer I had met earlier. He looked up, pointed a stubby finger in my direction and resumed reading what looked like some sort of logbook. Noisy. *Extremely* noisy.

This was my first chance to explore my new towboat home, the MV *Albert E. Heekin*, after coming aboard a couple of hours earlier. We were underway, shoving our tow of loaded coal barges up the Illinois River just upstream from Joliet. Five or six steps down from the main outer deck hallway—as in a split-level house—and off to my left, was the kitchen and dining area, or galley, as it is called on a boat. I peered into the crowded space, painted a glossy white and crammed with stainless steel cooktops, countertops, and serving areas. Very much a commercial setup. Frankly, I was relieved to see that it seemed much cleaner than the rest of the towboat.

Maybe once upon a time the *Albert E. Heekin* was a handsome vessel, but years of indelicate, lumbering operation, scraping and banging in the absurdly tight confines of the limestone-walled canals along the route into and out of Chicago had beaten her into cowed submission. Constantly moving barges filled with high-sulfur, filthy Southern Illinois coal forced coal dust and grime into every corner and crack. While the rivers across America were being cleaned up, the nasty Illinois River at that time had yet to be cleansed of the residue from serving as a sewer for millions for decades. Overall, a dirty, and I mean *dirty* environment.

So, she was what she was. I wished for the *Albert E. Heekin* a prouder existence. She was my very first towboat. But facts were facts. Not unlike a simple railroad freight car or city bus, this towboat operated relentlessly in the most hostile of environments, and unlike some of her more fortunate sister towboats, she was unlikely to ever see any improvement.

"Lookin' for something?"

The voice startled me as I looked around, exploring the galley. Like my cabin, we were slightly below the waterline. I could hear and feel the vibration of machinery close by. This part of the towboat was immediately above the furiously turning, massive propeller shafts. There was the unmuted sound of propellers close by as well as the sound of water churning.

"A water fountain or something like that?" I said.

"Broke. Ain't run in years. There's a pitcher of ice water in the fridge. You got something to put it in?"

"No, sir. I am afraid I don't." I moved toward him with my out-stretched hand. "Hi, my name is Tom. Just got on board. My first towboat."

Deckhand *catching a line* on the head of a towboat.

"Hi, Tom. I'm Jerry. Welcome aboard."

Jerry's smile was very slight but still nice and warm. He stuck out his pale, freckled hand and I shook it. His non-grip was a little creepy but adequate. He was dressed head to toe in white, five foot ten, skinny to the point of pants falling off, and his mutton chop sideburns were beginning to gray. Only one side of his smile curved up, and his long-overdue-to-be-trimmed eyebrows caused his striking light blue eyes to stand out even more.

"Under the cupboard there's a collection of jugs that have been left here. Pick one out and use it if you want."

I headed for the cupboard he'd indicated.

"You hungry?"

Jerry pulled hard on the handle of the stainless steel refrigerator behind him and opened the door wide, revealing all sorts of cold cuts, salad fixings, cheeses, and giant pitchers with labels like "tea" and "sweet tea" and "H2O." I didn't know what my timeline was for getting back out on the tow, so I respectfully declined.

"Hope yer a good eater! I got lots ready for supper!" Again, that simple but warm and kind smile. It felt good to think that with all the unknowns in this unfamiliar environment that this cook was being friendly to me, the new guy.

I grabbed what seemed to be the cleanest of the orphaned thermoses, rinsed it well with hot water from the large commercial sink, and filled it with ice water.

"Yer gonna be glad to have that out there **making the lock** comin' up," Jerry said.

making the lock – the process of performing deckhand duties while the tow goes through a lock. Tending lines, etc.

64

Photo of deckhand with bumper on the head of the tow while making a lock.

I walked upstairs then forward along the **guard** running the length of the towboat, and I could hear the second mate, Jim, cussing up another blue streak.

"Those sons a bitches put a pump away again without fillin' it with gas first, and I'm gonna fire somebody's ass! I talk and talk, but they don't pay me no nevermind, them sons a bitches!"

Jim and I had become new workmates only a couple of hours earlier, and I already knew three things about him. He seemed in a hurry to "get off this damn old river," his brutally callused never-seen-gloves hands looked like a war zone, and he didn't hesitate to swear.

"We got a pretty good **leaker**. These poor old beat to shit nasty old Valley Line junker barges don't ever git a break! Lazy-ass pilots drag 'em along these limestone walls and never even try to get off 'em. Good thing is it's right here on the stern next to the boat, so you and I don't need to drag this pump all over hell."

As he was explaining all this, he was topping off the pump's gas tank, sending him into another tirade.

guard - walkway along side walls longitudinally on sides of a towboat.
leaker - barge worn out from age or abuse that constantly leaked water into compartments.

65

"Damn! That pisses me off! One of these days I'm gonna.... Well, don't just stand there! Get ahold of the other end of the handle here!"

We lifted and carried the three-inch pump across the head deck of the towboat, and Jim climbed out onto the barge, helping me lower it into place next to the open *hatchway* on the back of the barge. I was startled to look down into the opening and see the water level in the barge just a little below the level of water in the river.

We got a bucket, and Jim showed me where and how much water to dump into the pump to prime it. Two quick starter pulls and the motor burst to life. A half a minute later a generous three-inch-wide column of water was shooting horizontally across the barge deck, washing trash and coal dust into the river. Our tow that day was eight loaded coal barges. Two barges wide and four barges long. Coming from a *fleet area* in Joliet up a narrow stretch of river to be delivered to the coal-fired power plants in metro Chicago.

Immediately in front of the open pilothouse front window, I could hear the captain talking to the lock on the radio. Booming loud. Lazy, a bit unintelligible, Southern Illinois slang.

"Bring her up onto the lower *guide wall* when you git up here. We got some debris we're trying to clear above the upstream *lock chamber valve*, so it will be a bit. We'll git to you quick as we can, over."

"Anybody southbound?" our captain asked the lockman.

"Nope. You're the only one around for the time being."

I glanced up at the captain, standing for the moment, centered behind the large pilothouse window. We made eye contact, and he grinned a bit.

hatchway – opening typically with watertight door for access into watertight compartments of a barge.
fleet area - place where barges are stored between movements.
guide wall - long reinforced concrete wall above and below the lock chamber that helps guide the tow into the lock without incurring damage.
lock chamber valve - operated by a lockman, allows water into or out of the lock chamber.

"Whaddaya think of this fine old rattrap of a vessel? Bet you didn't think it was gonna be like this…'" He spoke into a microphone on the end of a column hanging from the ceiling. A laugh, and then he looked ahead, not actually interested in a dialogue but in extending a captain-like welcome to me. Felt kind of good to be recognized by a real-life towboat captain. Wow.

"Come on. Git your shit and come on. I'll take you out to the head and show you how this is done," Jim said. As we walked down the center between the two *strings* of barges, I asked Jim about the quarter-inch-thick plastic-coated wire I hadn't noticed earlier.

"Oh, that's just *speaker wire*," Jim said. "We talk to the pilothouse from the head of the tow when we're making a full locking. If we have only a few barges, we kin git by with hand signals, but usin' a *speaker box* is better."

Photo of deckhand talking to pilothouse
using a speaker box on the bow of the tow.

string - slang for a single line of barges in front of the towboat; "two strings" means the tow is two barges wide
speaker wire - the wire from the speaker box to the pilothouse
speaker box - a speaker in a box on the head of the two that has a microphone to communicate with the pilothouse

As we walked the last 100 feet or so out onto the large bow area of the tow, I could see the ten-story-tall lower lock gates of Lockport Lock looming ahead. I had seen locks and dams on the Mississippi around home but nothing that tall and intimidating. Jim immediately began discussing strategy with the captain, talking into the speaker box and announcing our proximity to the lock wall.

"We'll git a headline and then *jackknife*, right? One thousand feet below, and yer *starboard side* is lined up dead on, Captain."

Upbound eight-barge tow on the Illinois River that could jackknife.
Currently configured to be a *set-over single locking*.

jackknife - process where a tow two barges wide and four barges long is changed to three barges wide and three long for lock
starboard side - right-hand side of towboat, barge, or tow looking forward
set-over single locking- this means the towboat could simply disengage from the tow and "set-over" to the port side and into that space shown on the photo. The boat would stay there while the eight barges were locked up or downstream as a single locking and then face back up where currently located after locking.

68

"Yeah. 'Cordin' to the lockman, we gotta wait. So git a line on the wall and then we'll jackknife," came the captain's response out of the speaker box. Pretty neat how that worked. *Must be a microphone hidden in there somewhere.*

"Jist a little more than eight hundred feet to go," Jim said.

I followed Jim's eyes and looked over to see large signs on the bank displaying numbers every hundred feet, and it became clear that Jim was not crystal-balling the distance—the signs were there to help make a safe approach. After lots more speaker talk back and forth, the captain stopped the 11,000-plus-ton tow precisely next to the timber-head on the lock wall. Jim wrapped the thick, dirty rope around and around, making several passes between the timberhead on the lock wall and the one on the front bow corner of the tow.

"C'mon," Jim muttered.

I dutifully followed, fascinated by every new thing I was seeing. We went toward the towboat, and at the coupling where we'd last tightened the rigging, Jim picked up a maul. He swung that sledgehammer quickly about eight times, and in a flash all the rigging we had worked to tighten was unhooked. One loud, explosive, reverse tension impact of his hammer at the connection for each set of rigging.

"Jist watch what I'm doin' 'cause this has all gotta be separated and placed just so. Be lots easier to put it back together when ya pay attention to how it gets taken apart!"

I felt helpless and a little frustrated. How was I supposed to make a good first impression if I couldn't hustle and help with this work? At the same time, I began to see some artistry to the way Jim was segregating the equipment and arranging the unhooked wires and rigging sets. In a bit I saw how to help, and without permission I was handling wires and actively disassembling the second coupling equipment before we performed the jackknife repositioning of the barges. I caught a hint of a grin on Jim's face as he watched me without comment.

Deckhand handling lockline during locking operations

I was determined to earn my place as part of the crew as quickly as I could.

To jackknife an eight-barge tow, the most forward of two couplings is disconnected and the barges are shifted and temporarily repositioned to make the tow three barges wide and three barges long. Then when the tow is secured in the lock chamber, the towboat shifts over into the empty space and the towboat and barges are locked through in one movement.

Water being discharged on the downstream side of the gates of an Illinois River lock.

My first time seeing anything like that, I was spellbound by the ease with which the captain moved the barges and how it all seemed so instinctive. When the tow was ready to be shoved into the lock chamber three across, Jim told me to stand by the headline on the bow corner. It was a few hours into my first watch on my first towboat and my first break. Continuing to take it all in, I noticed that the water immediately in front of us was disturbed. Then it was really roiling. The tow moved a bit, and the heavy rope between our tow and the lock guide wall snapped repeatedly with the strain. *Slap, tap, slap, crack.*

I wasn't sure everything was okay but heard no instructions from the speaker box, so I continued to watch.

It became obvious that the water was being released from the lock somewhere far below the surface immediately in front of our tow. Great volumes of foamy suds began to move in modest circles over the turbulence on the water, and before long the foam was four, then six, then perhaps eight feet deep. I was dumfounded. The pungent odor of the river water was even more pronounced, now heavily agitated and indirectly aerated. Jim showed up, and I asked what caused the foam.

"Jist know that if you fall in this here river, you are goin' directly to the hospital for a tetanus shot," he stated very matter-of-factly. "It's lots cleaner today than years ago. When I started out here, the foam would get so deep when they dumped the chamber that the pilot couldn't see me on the head of the tow!"

The swirls on the water diminished and then stopped altogether before the massive gates moved away from us and into the *recesses of the lock chamber walls*. A horn sounded on the lock wall, and the captain answered with a blast from our towboat's whistle.

From the speaker box, "Turn 'er loose, boys!"

I loosened the knot and unwound the *wraps* of that lengthy line from the shore timberheads, and into my first lock chamber we proceeded.

What a day!

---

recess in lock chamber wall - recess where the lock gates retreat when a lock gate is opened, making the surface of the walls flush
wrap - to wind a line around a timberhead or cavel/kevel several times before making a knot so the knot can be easily untied

"Anything else that stood out? What about living conditions aboard towboats?"

"Holy cow—the food! I could not believe the tremendous array of choices and the exquisite quality of every meal. Luxurious, home-cooked from scratch everything. Even when it is not mealtime there are readily available offerings of every snack, lunch meat, chips, and desserts that anyone could ever want."

Chapter 7
What About Those Keebler Elves?

I couldn't believe what was before me.

Is this how we would always eat?

I had just finished my first watch aboard the MV *Albert E. Heekin*, and we were beginning the afternoon/evening meal. Piles and more piles of potatoes and vegetables and meat and more meat.

Incredible.

Jerry, our cook, stood watch over the *galley* table. He smiled that cautious smile that I would learn was common among towboat cooks. All they wanted was to be appreciated. They didn't *need* acknowledgment, but they *loved* it! I would come to understand that every towboat cook was an invaluable part of the dynamic of day-to-day life aboard all towboats, but for that moment I was just stunned.

Jerry was no longer a youngster. Maybe sixty, unkempt graying hair with pale, loose skin under watery eyes in a pale face with a couple days' growth of a sparse set of whiskers. Long-sleeve plaid shirt under a white apron spotted with places where he'd wiped his hands. Sneakers flecked with flour and tan polyester work pants. He limped when he moved about the brightly lit workspace crammed with cast-iron grills and cooled by jumbo ceiling fans.

I lost my mom when I was very young and because of that I was the biggest fan *ever* of the school lunch lady. Anyone who cooked a real meal for me was top of the heap. Unlike most schoolkids, when that robust, handsome, but occasionally haggard gal spooned whatever that day's incredible goulash-like substance was onto my compartment tray, I grinned with all my might and praised her and thanked her. That got me at least a double helping, and I never forgot how welcome that simple, courteous acknowledgment was.

Deckhand shown here tossing a line across to another barge.

galley - a centrally located area on a towboat where food is prepared, served, and available around the clock. (kitchen, dining room)

I wasn't privy to Jerry's professional resume, but it didn't matter. I recognized the same scenario: a skilled human being with the ability to create pleasing, flavorful food that satisfied a need in a commercial setting. Female or male, these towboat savants served mostly unappreciative coworkers. I, however, amazed by the broad selection and subsequently discovered quality, was in awe of the vast variety of entrees for that day's p.m. meal.

The galley on the *Heekin* was on the main deck in the rear and was about twenty feet square. One wall was lined with cupboards filled with sturdy, restaurant china, and there were well-worn chairs around a table that sat eight comfortably. All the food was in the center of the table and was presented homestyle. Jerry smiled broadly as I fussed over the offerings and filled my first plate to overflowing. Lots of self-important murmuring among the others at the table. I was too new to be included. Didn't matter. If this was what towboat life was like, I wanted it all, completely and without reservation. Every bite I took was more incredible than the one before. *Holy crap! Is the food on towboats like this every meal?*

I watched as everyone cleared their own dishes, cup, and silver to the staging area adjacent to the commercial sinks. Shelves in that area were filled with snacks. Big side-by-side refrigerator with glass doors showing bowls of fruit, pies, cakes, and pitchers of drinks. Ice machine on the next counter over. Clearly this area was used for between-meal treats around the clock. A large part of that space was given over to shelves with nothing but dozens of packages of Keebler cookies.

I was told sometime later that a company called Chromalloy owned both the Valley Line Company and Keebler Cookies. Whether that was true or not, every Valley Line towboat had cupboards full of Keebler cookies. I ate more packages of Keebler French Vanilla Creme sandwich cookies than was probably wise on every Valley Line boat I ever rode.

"*Djyagitenough?*" Jerry asked as I moved my plate, cup, and silver over toward the sink area.

Djyagitenough - Did you get enough?

I couldn't help goggling at his commercial cooking area. Everything was stainless steel, and he had four individual ovens plus three big cooktops that I could see.

"Sure did. I am stuffed. You are really a good cook! I haven't eaten a meal like that in forever. Is it always like this?"

"Oh … you like the towboat food, then? You're really gonna like tomorrow night. Saturdays are always steak night on the boats."

"Oh, wow! That is sure to be wonderful! Have you been out here a long time?"

"Jist about ten years. Next month'll be my ten-year anniversary with the Valley Line. Good company. I bin on lots better boats than this old scow, but I go where they tell me ta go."

MV Albert Heekin
On the Illinois River at Hennepin, Illinois.

"This is my first boat. Just shipped out of the hall. Only had to wait eleven days. Friend of mine brought me down in the winter and got me registered. That whole eleven days I had the most senior **D Card**, so it was just a matter of waiting for a job nobody else wanted."

D card - the entry level of registration at the union to obtain a deckhand job.

The loud noises in the galley had increased now that the *Albert E. Heekin* was *faced up* and beginning to shove our eight loaded barges out of Lockport Lock. The unmistakable propeller propulsion racket began again underneath us at the stern of the towboat.

"Here. Lemme give ya some linens."

Jerry opened a locked door right off the galley. Inside were floor-to-ceiling shelves piled with white cotton sheets, pillowcases, and towels, some still enveloped in the stretch plastic wrap the commercial launderers had used.

"Ya git fresh stuff once a week on Saturday, so this will be yours for this comin' week till a week from tomorrow. I'll give ya an extra towel 'cause they're so damn small on this boat."

"All the rooms on this fine vessel down below the waterline?"

"Captain, pilot, the chief engineer, and my rooms are up in front and up top," Jerry responded.

"Little creepy looking out the window near the ceiling right out onto the surface of the river."

"Well, one good thing, probably makes the room a little cooler right there in front of the engine room. Yer air conditioner work in that room? The one they got in my room ain't worth a shit."

"I wasn't in there long enough to know. We'll see. Should I set my alarm clock? Is that how we get up for the next watch?"

"Somebody will come by and turn on your light at eleven thirty. If you want earlier, you gotta tell somebody."

faced up - the process of positioning and then fastening the towboat with multiple flexible-steel cables to the barges to be towed

I thanked Jerry again and headed forward past the engine room and down the steps coming to the T in the hallway.

Opening the door, I felt once more a bit of angst about spending time sleeping aboard this working towboat in a minuscule, noisy room down below the river surface. *Guess I'll get used to it.* I did do a couple of impromptu safety drills that included practicing moving along a safe route quickly up to the top decks. Made me feel immensely better about it.

I made up the top bunk and stored some of my gear in two of the four large metal lockers. They were the kind you used in high school, but one had shelves floor to ceiling. I hadn't met my bunkmate yet, but he kept his stuff and his bed very neat. I was glad for that. He worked the watch when I was off duty, one of the three other deckhands. The bath and shower area smelled of fresh soap, something like Irish Spring. That smell helped make my small, noisy, rather warm metal room a bit more pleasant as I hit the sack.

Before I knew it, I dozed off while reading. Peaceful and smiling, I woke up long enough to turn the reading light off and say some serious prayers of thanks for this dream come true.

A job on a towboat. Wow!

Deckhand shown here tending lock line during locking operations.

"Did it all just work out in the beginning? Any bumps in the road?"

"I was in heaven. I was learning how to make a life as an adult; my first 'real' job. I did have one incident. I bought a handsome, always-dreamed-of, used Jeep Wagoneer. I saw it as my new RV. I arrived in Joliet late one day, planning to ship out of the hall the next morning. Out of money, I searched for an 'off-road' location at the edge of metro Joliet to camp for the night. I ended up walking two miles to the nearest all-night truck repair business to borrow and lug several chains and a chain hoist back to the woods, where I spent all night yanking my stuck-up-to-the-axles RV out of the soft soils I didn't notice when I parked there."

Chapter 8
Conditional Acceptance?

"What!?? Who's there!??"

Seemed like I had only been asleep for a couple of minutes before there was a knock on the door, and the overhead light turned on. Yikes. *Did I request this wake-up call?*

Fog lifting a little, I began to hear the insistent noise and vibration that I had successfully blocked a few hours before at the beginning of my brief sleep. Yawning, I turned and thought a bit about how I would successfully negotiate my descent from the top bunk as an adult. Seemed like there was nothing to it when I was a youngster. I swung around and down. The slick tile floor was pleasantly warm. I kind of felt like a camper or maybe a would-be explorer as I made up my bed after my first towboat sleep. I noted the crisp fragrance and stark whiteness of the bedding as I arranged it neatly. Such a sharp contrast to the general unkempt condition of the towboat quarters, but I didn't spend a lot of time pondering the dissimilarity.

I reached into my locker for my clothes and began to dress. Noisy. Considerable amounts of noise. *This must be the way it always is.* Vibration and the sounds of motors and equipment grinding and purring.

The door opened again and shut, just like that. *Must also be a normal routine aboard a towboat.* Whoever gets to wake folks up prior to the next watch makes a second pass just to be sure everybody is up and at 'em. Interesting. Fascinating, really.

Sheer limestone walls line the canal portion
of the Upper Illinois River at Lemont, Illinois.

Waking up a little more, I was restless and excited to continue learning how this towboat thing was going to go. Finished dressing and tidying up, I left my room and climbed the stairs for the first nighttime shift of my towboat career. I sensed that we had stopped moving upstream, and a look at the nearby limestone riverbank confirmed that. I got some water in the galley and grabbed a generous hunk of bologna, also called "horse cock" on towboats, from the extraordinary selection Jerry maintained for crew member snacks in that giant commercial refrigerator.

As I moved forward along the guard of the narrow towboat, I noted the numerous floodlights all over, strategically stationed to illuminate everything within fifty yards of the towboat. It was bright as day. I reached the head deck and grabbed the same not-quite-the-worst-looking life jacket I wore the day before. I adjusted it a little more snugly to take advantage of the modest warmth it supplied in the just after midnight cool.

The towboat was tied up next to two rows of loaded coal barges moored side by side at the Commonwealth Edison power plant just downstream from Lemont, Illinois. Colossal, towering buildings that were decades old and almost all dilapidated, filthy, and decaying. Located right on the edge of the river, the largest were turn-of-the-century—now abandoned—factories or steel-making structures that used to house huge furnaces and tall cranes.

"We got a couple more sets of rigging to *strip off* here, and then we're moving to the next coupling. Git the hell out of the way or pitch in and grab some here!" Cliff, the mate on the forward watch, was a crabby old bastard. He wore a permanent scowl and seemed determined to be off-color with every word he spoke.

The mate on my watch was much friendlier. Even though I was new, Jim had made me feel welcome and mostly accepted the previous afternoon. He walked out onto the tow, now in charge, as Cliff walked

Strip off or *strip the tow* - process of removing rigging (wires, ratchets, lock lines, etc.) from the barges onto the towboat

off and onto the towboat without a word. Satisfied that our equipment was all on board, Jim told me to untie the boat, and we moved to the next coupling.

"Gotta git you a flashlight, Tommy. You got gloves?"

I nodded.

There was a small deck locker right off the head deck filled with running lights and miscellaneous crew supplies: rain gear, flashlights, batteries, something called a *fid*. Jim pulled out a new flashlight and dropped fresh batteries in it. Handing it to me, he said, "Try to keep track of this. Cliff gits all out of sorts when anybody loses one. It's like he bought 'em himself!"

Meanwhile, the pilot had moved the towboat 200 feet to where the next two sets of barges were coupled together.

Jim handed me a sledgehammer. "Look here. Notice the very end of this ratchet. The hooked thing is called a 'pelican hook.' This ring that slides up to and over the end of it is called a *keeper* hook because

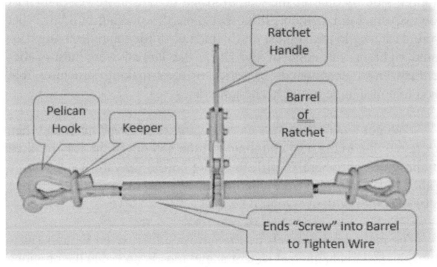

Rachet components.

fid - like the barrel of a bat and narrowing to a point, a wooden tool used to splice lines
keeper - oblong steel ring that secures the end of the ratchet connected to the wire or strap

it keeps the ratchet connected to the wire. Always be sure when you knock the keeper off with the hammer that your feet are well away 'cause sometimes they just explode apart!"

He took the sledge from me and with a deft swing hit the keeper of the first ratchet we came to and then handed the hammer to me. I was stunned at how much energy was released as the rigging holding the barges into a tow was unhooked. Jim motioned that I should continue this process with the remaining ratchets at that coupling. Executing his duties as the after watch deck crew manager meant mostly directing. The deckhands, Ray and I, did all the actual work.

We coiled up the oily one-inch flexible-steel cables that criss-crossed between the barges securing them to one another. When that was complete, the cables, the ratchets, and any remaining equipment was gathered up and stored on the *head deck* of the towboat. Once we completed stripping the tow, we reversed the process by passing that equipment out onto our downbound tow of empties.

Two coiled-up piles of lock lines on the head of a tow.

head deck - work area at the bow of a towboat that usually includes bits and winches for facing up

"Gimme the tail of that *lock line* so I can wrap it around the capstan here."

I wasn't sure which one was the lock line, but I must have guessed correctly. This process of *building tow* was cool.

Jim took the remainder of the lock line and made a circle around four timberheads, one on each abutting corner of the first four barges we were to fasten together. Easing down the steps of the *tow knee* back on the head deck of the towboat, he flipped the wall-mounted switch that started the *capstan* turning.

Capstan on the head-deck of a towboat.

lock line - superior quality, very thick and usually long line used to moor while going through locks
building tow - the process of arranging the barges properly according to weight and type and wiring them together with rigging
tow knee - structure with vertical surface against the barge and stairs on the opposite side used to get up to the level of empty barges
capstan - large, circular, rotating timberhead-like tool around which one wraps a line that is used to pull the line in and secure it

Two deckhands connecting rigging in a coupling on a tow.

"C'mere, Tommy."

Watching and learning from Jim was like watching a maestro conduct an orchestra. Effortlessly, he wrapped that thick rope (called a *line* on the river) three times around the capstan. As the capstan turned, he varied the pressure on the line. A capstan is either on or off. It has a powerful electric motor, but there is no way to adjust how hard it pulls or how fast it goes. So when Jim wanted to pull the line to press the barges together, he simply tugged the line a bit, holding pressure, and it gripped the capstan while it was spinning. When Jim got the line as tight as it could be, he turned the capstan off and made the line fast by synching it down on the fitting on the side of the capstan.

line - Commonly known as a rope, a river line needs to be able to hold hundreds of tons and is usually between two and four inches in circumference. Modern lines are almost all some form of polyethylene and/or nylon.

"Git that riggin' laid out like it was 'fore you picked it all up a while ago. Come git me when you got it, and I'll help you connect and tighten it."

I felt a sense of contentment and fulfillment out on the decks of those barges performing interesting, satisfying work that cool, fall early morning on the river. I was also very pleased that without any fanfare, Jim was mentoring me with minimal direction and demonstrated respect for my work ethic. My sense was that my chosen career fit like a glove.

Rigging in a coupling on an Illinois River coal tow.
At lower right is vertical electric powered pump that Valley Line used commonly.

"I have heard that Central Illinois can get hot and humid in the summer. Lots of farming, and it rains every day."

"Oh yeah. I spent so much time observing everything new that it didn't occur to me that it was hot. But it was. And the work was harder than any I had ever done. I just simply adapted. I loved it. If this was to be my new life, I needed to embrace it and enjoy it. And I did."

Chapter 9
Valley Line Illinois River Towboats

"It's damn hot out."

"Yep, it is."

"I shoulda took that Valley Line job today that was on the *two p.m. call* at the union hall."

Pete, a veteran deckhand who *shipped out* of the Joliet union hall regularly, was lamenting his decision to let that job pass. I was enjoying listening to him and a couple of other deckhands sitting at the bar at Johnny's. It was a hot June Thursday, and the Schlitz Beer sign on the brick façade just up the street from the union hall had drawn me in. I was new to Joliet and to working on the river and was intrigued at the idea of learning new things from seasoned colleagues.

"Hi, I'm Tom."

2:00 p.m. call - Deckhand jobs were printed (posted) on a board at the union hall in Joliet, Illinois, each weekday at 8:30 a.m., 10:30 a.m., and 2:00 p.m.
ship out - slang for taking one of the jobs posted at the union hall in Joliet.

"I'm Pete."

"I'm drunk and name's Stan," the tallest one said.

"I'm Cliff, and I'm damn glad not to have taken that Valley Line job."

"Why's that?" I asked. I motioned to the bartender to set us up with another round of beers.

"You get down there at **Kingston Mines** this time of year buildin' tow, and damn, they ain't a breath of air in that godforsaken valley!"

Pete raised his bottle and Cliff clinked his against it in a classic, symbolic toast.

"I know what you mean!" Cliff said after a long swallow of beer. "Last summer I was on the *Dresden* for eighty-eight days straight, and we were in there every four days makin' tow. It was hell."

Wow. Eager to learn all the ins and outs of local towboat work, I asked some questions that surely gave me away as a greenhorn.

"So you guys are saying that the Valley Line jobs on the board at the union hall should be avoided?"

"Naw, they ain't that bad," Pete responded.

"Just that you gotta be up to it. Good steady work, them jobs. Twelve up and twelve down. Sometimes fifteen. They all layin' together at **Grundy County Fleet**, and ya jist gotta rig 'em up and head south."

Kingston Mines - facility on the Illinois River where coal mined in Central Illinois is loaded into barges
Grundy County Fleet - location on the Illinois River where Valley Line barges were kept in a fleet and where towboats took on supplies & made crew changes

Grundy County Fleet was located under the Interstate Highway 80 bridge
along the east shore of the Illinois River in Joliet, Illinois.

"Gittin' the tow built downriver is another thing. But, jist a watch or two, and then ya got three days of upbound lockin' and runnin' time agin. Them boats is nice boats with good air-conditionin' and damn good cooks."

I felt like I had stumbled into a gold mine of insight. There was little information shared around the union hall; folks were just there to see what jobs were available and to sign on. It seemed like a good idea to learn as much as I could about the work and working conditions for each of the companies that procured deckhands there.

"I'mona git out tomorrow if another Valley Line job comes in. 'Bout outta money."

MV *Brandon*, Valley Line Illinois River line-haul coal towboat.
One of authors favorites.

Pete was a very peaceful sort with one of those great smiles augmented by dentures. He had long ago become a senior citizen, and his slight frame did not give him away automatically as a riverman. I asked him more about the various companies hiring from the union hall.

"You seen it there. I bin there when you was there. Material Service has jobs. They got nice boats, but small. Yellow and red. Sand and such up into the city. Back and forth, back and forth. Up here from Lockport, up into Chicago, and back out. Twenty-one days they work. ***Twenty-one on, twenty-one off instead of thirty days***.

"Twin City Barge. They got good jobs. Small boats too, but good accommodations, good cooks, and easy work. Four, five barges in and out. Easy tow makin' and mostly ***regulars***. Not very often them jobs come to the hall. You gotta be lucky to git out with them."

"So Valley Line, Material Service, and Twin City Barge. They are the three hiring at the hall?" I asked.

"Let's you 'n me git us a Valley Line boat tomorrow, Tom. Whaddaya say?"

Twenty-one on, twenty-one off instead of thirty days - two common towboat deck assignments of twenty-one days or thirty days
regular - as in "regular employee" working primarily for that one barge company

"If a couple jobs come in, I'm with ya, Pete."

We raised a toast, clicked our Schlitz bottles together, and with that charming smile of his, we forged an agreement.

The following afternoon, sure enough, three deckhand jobs were posted at the 2:00 p.m. call for the MV *AM Thompson*. The *Thompson* was the largest of the Illinois River Valley Line coal tow-boats.

"Gimme and the kid here two of them spots, George."

"They want ya down to Grundy County soon as ya kin git there. Headin' southbound this afternoon."

"We'll hightail it right down there, George. See ya next trip!"

Illinois River line-haul coal towboat MV *AM Thompson*.

A little bit of paperwork and we were on our way. I asked Pete if I could walk to Grundy County because I didn't know if I had enough money to split a cab.

"I got the cab, kid. You can git the next one."

Arriving under the Interstate Highway 80 bridge crossing the Illinois River, we were left down low and behind a monstrous

concrete revetment holding the river in place. We trudged up the ramp with our bags, all the while listening to the din of traffic crossing the bridge.

I was astonished by the size of the MV *AM Thompson*. Oh, my goodness. The largest of Valley Line's towboats running the Illinois, she seemed supersized compared to the *Albert E. Heekin*, my most recent assignment. I immediately fell in love. Hadn't I dreamed of working these mammoth towboats as a youngster watching them go by Prescott? I couldn't believe it was real. A bunch of the crew welcomed Pete aboard, and it already seemed like I'd make the right choice as I moved stealthily along in the draft of his experienced, familiar presence.

"Them rooms on here are dandies. Yer gonna like 'em."

We hauled our bags down the side deck of the vessel, dodging the face wires and various deck fittings. Entering the cool, polished, clean hallway toward the interior, I couldn't help comparing this towboat to the *Heekin*. No wonder the crew on the *Heekin* had such disdain for that vessel. The *Thompson* smelled like all work boats, for sure, but cleaner—a strong scent like Lysol or some similar industrial-strength cleaning solution. All the floors, walls, and light fixtures were unusually clean. Not what I had become accustomed to.

Line-haul coal towboat upbound near Ottawa, Illinois.

concrete revetment - assorted designs of concrete structures constructed to be the "bank" of an existing river.

Pete showed me the door to my room and told me to meet him out on deck in five minutes. I was stunned when I opened the door. My room had a desk and two chairs alongside the metal lockers, with a sink, stool, and shower right there. Very cool air was flowing freely from the window air conditioner, and it was bright, very clean, and tidy. *This is for me!*

I dressed quickly in my work clothes, expecting to be on watch or ready to be so since it was very close to 6:00 p.m. I entered the hallway just as Pete did, and together we headed for the forward deck.

"You are a damn nice sight for an old bastard like me! Thought I'd never see an experienced deckhand again!" the crewman on deck called out as soon as he saw us.

It was clear that Johnny, the second mate, knew Pete well and liked him. The feeling was mutual, and they shook hands, smiled, and chit-chatted.

"The kid here's gonna be okay too. He's a good one, I reckon."

Johnny shook my hand, and I felt an immediate sense of relief and welcome. *Can it get any better than this?*

"We're gittin' fuel and water, so you guys can git situated and relax. Tow is built. All they gotta do is face up and head south. Git your sheets from the cook, and git yer beds made up and git ready for supper."

I followed Pete aft, and we entered the galley through a side door. Roomy, bright, and again, much cleaner than the galley on board the *Albert E. Heekin.* The cook shook Pete's hand and got us each sets of linen and towels and said to be back for supper soon.

Pete looked at me and smiled. "Told ya you'd like this boat, didn't I?"

I smiled broadly. "I am grateful, Pete, for everything. Wow. I really like this boat. I hope I can fit in with this crew. Thanks for helping me get here and making me feel so welcome. I promise I will be a hard worker, and you'll be proud to have recommended me."

"I like ya, kid. Not a problem."

I won the assignment of daily cleaning of the pilothouse on the MV *Thompson*.
I enjoyed looking out the pilothouse windows
at our fifteen loads of coal upbound on the Illinois River.

"Tell me a little about the work of a deckhand. It seems like it might be dangerous."

"Yes, it is a dangerous and very industrial setting. Huge, heavy barges and crude steel tools fastening barges together. Narrow walkways and work areas. Falling into the river or between barges is always on your mind. And the constant movement is almost hypnotic. The tow is always on the move. Fun seeing the different things along the riverbanks as you passed."

Chapter 10
Hardest Work I Ever Encountered

The massive chain links scraped across three barges before I summoned all the strength I had to throw the three *chain-link straps* across the head deck of the *Thompson*. The temperature was somewhere north of ninety degrees just after noon at the Kingston Mines rail-to-barge coal transshipment terminal in Havana, Illinois. Eighteen years old, six foot two, 250 pounds, I was a healthy, young kid, and I was thrilled to be there. The hardest work I had ever done, but all new and interesting.

chain-link straps - primarily used to connect the anchor end of the ratchet to a fitting on a barge

"Slow down, kid. You ain't gonna make the whole afternoon if you don't pace yerself. Had a green kid go down on me here last trip, and he wasn't no good resta the trip." Johnny, the second mate, had had a new deckhand collapse with heat exhaustion.

"Be damn sure to take some of these every hour or so." Pete, my fellow deckhand on the after watch, handed me two white pills. "Them is salt pills. Keeps ya hydrated."

I watched Pete work, and I noticed that he moved steadily but far from quickly. Nonetheless, we were both soaked completely to the skin with sweat after only the first hour of the afternoon watch. We had two more *couplings* to go before the tow was ready to head upbound.

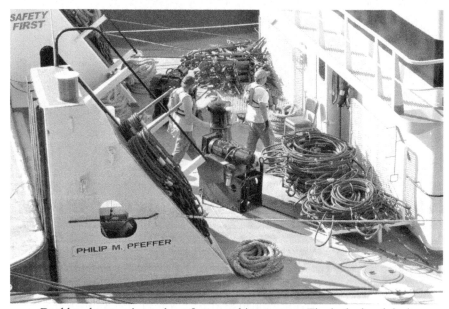

Deckhands returning to boat from working on tow. The is the head deck of line-haul towboat showing rigging stacked and stored.

The barges were moored three wide in the fleet waiting for us. The captain moved the huge 3,900-horsepower towboat along the river side of the barges, stopping where they were joined together end to end

couplings - connection made with rigging between barges forward and back and sideways with *lines*. Johnny and Pete worked together wrapping a thick rope this way and that among the fittings on the barges, eventually tightening the rope with the capstan when the barges were lined up for a perfect, tight fit.

I had seen this done on my last trip and wanted to help but understood that they had an unspoken, well-rehearsed method. I watched intently.

"We need four sets in each string. Complete sets. Wire, chain strap, and ratchet. Should end up with twelve sets, givertake."

Coal mined in various locations around Illinois is moved by train to Havana, Illinois, where it is loaded here into barges destined for power plants in Chicago.

Johnny was not much of a talker. His instructions were brief. He also moved steadily and with purpose. It occurred to me that he and Pete were experts in conserving energy by making every move count. Pete and I did most of the bull work, and Johnny was our shift leader.

What we were doing is called *building a tow*. A full *double-lock* line-haul tow is generally fifteen barges. At the locks, the first nine barges (three barges wide and three long) are locked through first. Once that is complete, the next six (three wide and two long) and the towboat

lines - ropes used to moor barges to docks or tie them together
building a tow - arranging the barges and fastening them together with rigging
double-lock - a tow larger than the typical lock chamber (600 feet long and 110 feet wide) that has to lock through in two phases

connected to them are locked through.

At each coupling, the barges are fastened together end to end and side by side. Flexible-steel cables, most about three-quarters of an inch to one inch in diameter, are wrapped around timberheads and assorted fittings during this process.

The rigging must hold the tow together so that it does not bend or flex in any way when transiting the river. The tool that tightens the cables used in the rigging is a ratchet. When the ratchet is turned, the ends are screwed into the center of the device, pulling the cables taut. Installing and tightening rigging is backbreaking, demanding work.

Note how all the rigging holds the tow of barges together side to side and end to end. Good example of scissor wires.

The decks of those older *hopper barges* loaded with coal were filthy with coal dust and hot. The afternoon wore on, and we eventually faced up the towboat to the tow. The day had been incredible, and I was exhausted.

"Ya did okay, kid. Yer gonna make it jist fine."

Pete nodded his agreement. We hung our life jackets on hooks in the mate's locker and headed aft to get cleaned up for supper.

hopper barges - barge that is designed to function without a cover

98

"Ya got a couple easier watches comin' now. We'll just be makin' locks fer a couple a days. That's the upside to these Valley boats. Fair 'mount of ridin' time."

"Thanks for your encouragement, Pete. I'm lovin' this."

Ratchets shown here hooked to chain straps and wires.

I cut my hair in the mirror in my room that night after supper with dull scissors and a toenail clipper. It was hot working on the decks of the barges, and I expected more of the same for weeks to come. Shorter hair, pretty or not, was sure to make a difference.

I had a brief but solid sleep. Midnight came, and when I stepped out onto the head deck I was greeted by the same humidity, but much cooler temperatures.

"What the hell'd ya do to yer hair?"

Johnny and Pete were smirking and shaking their heads. I smiled back self-consciously while they chuckled. We donned our life jackets and went out onto our tow, following the beams of our flashlights.

I was still getting used to the difference between the crappy old *Albert E. Heekin* and the *Thompson*. Even at three times the power, the *Thompson* was so spacious that the sound and vibration seemed substantially less. Additionally, the Illinois River there was dark and silent in contrast to the Upper Illinois, whose banks are filled cheek by jowl with lights, refineries, and constant industrial activity and noise. It was peaceful and serene as we progressed steadily upstream.

"Take yer time checkin' these crappy old hopper barges," Johnny told us when we reached the tow. "Them boys on the upper end just lay these beat-up barges up against the sheer limestone banks up there and grind along, rubbing any life they used to have out of 'em. It don't take that much to git 'em out in the channel, but they is just laaaazzzy!"

I had seen that in person while working aboard the *Heekin*. Frequently, the captain would just let the tow scrape along the limestone walls that lined the river on both sides from Joliet all the way upstream past Lemont on the way into Chicago.

Hatchways for checking and access individual water-tight tanks in barges
Note the stern tank hatch on this barge.

Pete and I acknowledged Johnny's directive and headed forward. Each barge has four individual watertight tanks and two end compartments. Every compartment has a hatchway on the surface of the barge, and each compartment was checked for water at the beginning of every watch by opening the hatch and looking around.

They almost always have some water in them, and anything more than ten or twelve inches is pumped out. Once the water is pumped out, the mate or a deckhand climbs down a ladder into the compartment to try to locate the source of the water. Bundles of cedar shingles are always part of the deck equipment. Water seeping through a slight crack in the steel hull of a barge can be stopped or slowed by driving a shingle into the crack. The damage is noted, and an appointment in the repair yard is made.

Author enjoying his experiences as a river deckhand.

Pete and I found three leakers and one stern ***crash box*** that was full of water to the level of the river.

crash box - square end of a barge engineered to withstand a crash without endangering the barge cargo

Lots of pumping and patching occurred on the tows, and Valley Line used vertical-shaft electric pumps. This was instead of heavy, awkward gasoline pumps and hoses that had to be lugged around. It was easy work moving along in the night.

Pete rolled his own cigarettes, and I watched in fascination while he did this perfectly in the dark. The light of the match showed his weary countenance. "Don't know how many more trips I kin make."

"How long you been out here, Pete?"

"I was deckin' down on the *Intracoastal* since I was a kid. Different deal, those boats. No cook, no time off, but didn't know no different. Made *tankerman* but could never git a license. Got off one of those tramp unit towboats up here fourteen years ago, and somebody mentioned the union hall. Best thing that ever happened to me. Never looked back. Been shippin' outta the hall ever since. I stay out more days at a time than most. Visit my sister down in Kentucky between trips and gotta gal friend down there. Not much to look at, but she's damn good in the sack. Got family back in Texas, and I make a couple a trips down there every winter.

"Wished I could git me a job on the Twin City Barge Line boats. Everybody says they are the best boatin' company. They got same *day-for-day* and union insurance and retirement. It'd be a little easier for this old man."

"They never have jobs that come through the union hall?"

"Only one that I ever seen, and I didn't take it 'cause I just got off with sixty days. I shoulda grabbed it, and maybe I coulda *got on steady with them*."

Intercoastal - the inland waterway that goes west from New Orleans adjacent to the Gulf of Mexico all the way to Mexico
tankerman - person trained and skilled at loading and unloading tank barges, frequently handling volatile fuels
day-for-day- one day off with pay for each day worked
got on steady with them - work exclusively for one towboat company and enjoy associated benefits, including seniority

"I wonder how people get the Twin City jobs." As we were talking, I kept us on task, moving the pumps and their electric cords.

"Reckon you gotta know somebody. That's what I heard. They kin hire anybody they want long as they git 'em to join the union."

"I'm gonna look into workin' for them. I live up in the St. Paul area, and I know they run boats there in the summer. I think they gotta main office there.

"Help me pullin' this pump outta here and down the way. We just about got these all done."

A few days later, I fell from the *gunwale* of an empty hopper barge about sixteen feet down into the bottom. I was just heading out onto the tow beginning my shift and not fully awake.

Gunwale of a hopper barge

The pilot blew the towboat's whistle several short blasts (I later learned that's the danger signal and he seemed very concerned over the loudspeaker about my well-being. No one was more surprised than me, and it was over in a second. Thankfully, I landed perfectly horizontally, and my entire body absorbed the blow rather easily.

gunwale - pronounced "gunnel," walkway down the side of a barge

I lay there in a couple of inches of rainwater and loose coal debris, catching my breath. I remember being mostly upset that my freshly laundered clothes were no longer clean. I got to my feet, checked my limbs, and felt fortunate to be unhurt. Pete lowered a ladder, and I climbed out.

"Ain't never seen that happen before. You okay? How come you din't break somethin'?"

"Aw, it's nothin'. I'm fine. Just dirty and wet. I landed just right. Guess I gotta be more careful, don't I"?

Pete smiled at me, shaking his head. "I been out here all these years and ain't never seen sumpin' like that where a man didn't get hurt. You must have a horseshoe jammed a long way up your ass!"

The laundry thing was completely new to me. I had been taking my clothes to a laundromat shoreside for years. Coins in, clean and dry clothes out. Towboat laundry equipment so far had been a series of very simple electric washtubs with a wringer on a pivot above. It took me a bit to figure it out. You fill the washer with water, soap, and clothes, and plug in it. The center agitator moves to and fro for a bit, and then you wring the wash water out of your clothes, drain the washer, and refill it with fresh rinse water. Let that work through the clothes and repeat, running things through the wringer and hanging them to dry. Most of the laundry setups had been next to the engine room—lots and lots of heat—so clothes hung on the clothesline there dry almost instantly.

The remainder of that trip was uneventful. I enjoyed my new deckhand role on a line-haul towboat. The locks were fascinating, and the creature comforts aboard the *Thompson* were much nicer.

On live-aboard towboats, the pilot's and captain's rooms and the pilothouse are cleaned daily by one of the crew. It paid a few extra dollars per day, and I jumped at the chance. No one said much about what to clean or how to clean the pilothouse or the officers' quarters, but I must have done okay. I was suddenly glad to have learned as a boy how to clean since I had no one to do it for me after my mother passed.

My first time up the stairs and into the expansive pilothouse was to clean it. I quietly and privately thought I might stop breathing. The pilot, named Steve, was a bearded, very cheerful character. Long-sleeve shirt hanging out, jeans, sneakers, and always a smile. He was standing at the console bent forward more than seemed healthy. His Southern drawl was so pronounced that I had to guess at what he was saying.

Captain at the *sticks*, steering a towboat on the river.

"Win'd you git on? 'Fore we headed downbound last trip? D'you get outta the hall? They sure 'nough sendin' us some dandies. Lotsa long-hair critters. Not sure what the hell that's all about. My gal said I grow my hair out, I gotta git out. Plain as that. All you damn kids got the long-ass hair…"

The second mate, Johnny, came upstairs to change the carbons

sticks - levers on the captain's console that swing side to side and move the towboat's rudders

in the giant *carbon arc searchlights* so they would be ready to go at dusk. He was impressed and pleased when I offered to clean the mirrors at the back of the awesome equipment. I really just wanted to check them out.

I spent all the time I could in the pilothouses without making a nuisance of myself or seeming too obvious. I felt privileged to be allowed this delightful extravagance. Intuitively, I was certain I would end up there, and I wanted to see and experience it all. The radios, the *sticks* he used to steer, the windows, all the switches, the radar, all amazing!

The way Steve was making the tow travel up and down the river was fabulous. Upbound, it looked like a breeze. Downbound was a different thing. The *Thompson* moved loaded coal barges upstream and empties downstream almost exclusively. The tow of empties seemed to fill the entire river from bank to bank in and around turns and tight spots.

"That's called 'sliding,'" Steve said one day when he caught me watching him. "Keeps you on yer toes. Kinda fun in the daylight. Nighttime, not so much. Don't know nothin' but this damn old river, and this what I do. You wanna be a pilot one day?"

More than you can ever imagine, sir. More than you can know.

carbon arc searchlights - intensely bright lights containing carbon rods that arc when electricity passes through them in front of convex mirrors

> "Eventually you ended up working on rivers other than the Illinois. Was that your plan? How did that occur?"

> "I got an assignment out of the Joliet union hall working on the MV *WS Rhea* over on the Upper Mississippi. The most spectacular, epic example of a premier line-haul towboat working the 'Upper' at that time."

Chapter 11
In Between

I spent the summer of 1970 working on boats I was assigned to from the union hall. Lots of Illinois River trips. The MV *Brandon*, the MV *Dresden*, the MV *Central*, and again aboard the MV *Thompson*. These were the best opportunities for a young man working as a deckhand on the river in Illinois.

Late that first summer, a job was posted to get aboard the MV *WS Rhea* over in Rock Island, Illinois. I couldn't believe it. I had never seen jobs on the Upper Mississippi (140 miles west) posted at the union hall in Joliet. Could this be the boat on the Upper Mississippi that would travel up and downstream past my hometown of Prescott, Wisconsin, on the Mississippi?

"You gotta way to git over to Rock Island?"

"You bet, George," I told him. "I can be there this afternoon."

I met her later that evening at Lock and Dam 15, northbound at Arsenal Island. The lock is on the edge of the island, also home to First Army Headquarters.

"Can I please keep my van here for a few weeks?"

The guy at the gate of the secure federal facility eyed me. "We don't normally do that, young man. But seein' as how you are gitten on a towboat here, I'll make a note in the log, and yer van will be okay here till ya git back."

Earlier that month I had purchased a new basic utility van, a vehicle I had dreamed about owning for years. I planned to travel and enjoy my youthful independence and generous time off with pay, and it was to be my entry-level recreational vehicle. I spent the better part of a week installing insulation and then a thin but sturdy layer of plywood to the interior of my brand-new 1970 Ford Econoline. Next, I put the finishing touch on the cocoon-like interior by stapling shag carpet sample pieces of various colors into place. I wired some very good quality speakers to the new, state-of-the-art, high-fidelity Panasonic combo FM/eight-track player. I installed a single bed, a chair, and a cooler, and my rig was completely set. I was happy to discover such a great safe place to leave my new toy.

Two hours later, the second half of the double-locking of the MV *WS Rhea* moved into the lock chamber, and I got aboard. I was immediately impressed beyond words.

She and her sister towboat, the MV *L. Wade Childress*, were the biggest and most powerful towboats on the Upper Mississippi River in those days. One hundred seventy-six feet long and forty feet wide, she was the most beautiful towboat I had ever seen. Lavish accommodations relatively speaking and throbbing power that left you in awe.

A proud, well-kept old girl from another generation, with all the latest upgrades. She was the premier and most prestigious vessel traveling the Upper Mississippi. I felt very privileged to be part of her crew.

MV *L. Wade Childress*, sister towboat to MV *WS Rhea*. Both ran the Upper Mississippi for the Valley Line Company.

Captain Norman Hillman welcomed me aboard. "Glad you could git here today. Don't normally git a deckhand outta the hall the same day I put in for one. You need to sign these papers that I gotta turn in to the office. "Shorty Turner is the mate on your watch, and I expect you to do as he tells you and to work hard here as part of our crew."

"You needn't worry, Captain. I'm thrilled to be able to work on this boat. I grew up in Prescott, Wisconsin, at Mile Point eight eleven point four, and I've watched you traveling past my whole life."

The pilothouse of the *WS Rhea* was like a monument to days gone by. Four stories high, spacious, and well-appointed. She had the feel of the giant steamers of the past but also had all the latest amenities. Two huge radar boxes were placed one on each side of the captain's console. There were expansive windows and gigantic carbon arc searchlights outside on the flybridge outside the pilothouse. When he noticed my interest, Captain Hillman showed me the areas on the console where the instrumentation was for the ***swing meter*** and the ***autopilot***. Pristine and shiny, this pilothouse was clearly special.

swing meter and autopilot - The captain could engage the autopilot to steer precisely in a straight line, controlled by the swing meter, very sophisticated technology for that time.

As I traveled down the outside deck aft toward my quarters, I stopped and marveled at the engine room. Two giant 2,800-horsepower engines. A crewman, who I later learned was called an *oiler*, spent all his work time just moving about and around those immense engines, lubricating moving parts and wiping down oily spill areas. Heat, noise, and mechanical energy unlike any I had experienced. Simply astounding.

I found my way to the galley and met the cook, Charlie Morris. He set me up with my linens and towels and pointed me in the direction of my quarters. At dinner that evening I met Shorty. He welcomed me and said to meet him on the head deck around midnight, and we would get our work assignments. I fell asleep quickly and slept briefly, thinking about my new work setting. Just before midnight I walked forward along the port side of the enormous boat.

Shorty met me and passed me my flashlight. "Pick one out that fits ya," he said, pointing toward a pile of dirty, well-used life vests, "and keep it with ya, so you always have it at the ready. We're gonna check the tow and meet back here after."

Same humid but cool night setting on the Upper Mississippi as along the Illinois River. Similar noises emanating from the engines of the boat and same brilliant, star-filled sky. Sometimes the pilot navigated without any searchlights, and it seemed like the whole universe was right above you, close enough to touch. The Milky Way was always visible. When the powerful carbon arc searchlights came on, you could follow the beam to where the pilot was looking and see, bright as day, the corner of the pier or dock, whatever was to be avoided while navigating. This was an entirely different kind of tow. No coal. Mostly barges loaded with salt going to Minnesota. Newer barges for sure, and we had six empties in our tow of fifteen barges.

"Shorty's a great guy. We do our job, he'll completely leave us alone. Bin workin' regular over here for little more than three years. You?" My fellow deckhand's name was Mark.

oiler - a worker on a towboat who monitors, attends to, and cleans the engine room

"I just started out in May. This is my first trip over on the Upper. Bin working coal boats over on the Illinois for Valley Line. Outta the hall."

"I like this river way better'n the Illinois. Them ol' coal boats is rats. Dirty, filthy, always pumpin' leakers. Amazin' that they don't lose more barges than they do! We almost never find a hatch with enough water in it to pump. Yer gonna like this.

"You take this string, and I'll take the other side," he added.

We walked out onto the tow checking each of the hatches as we moved forward. When barges are three wide in a tow, it's only necessary to check the hatches on the barges where they are side by side. The five watertight compartments along the length of a barge extend from one side to the other, so you never have to check hatches where you could accidentally slip into the river.

Head of the tow, location of running lights, lock lines, and depth-finding equipment.

The farther away from the towboat, the quieter. Closest to the head of the tow, the night noise becomes an occasional steel on steel squeak or rigging snapping with pressure from the captain steering the tow. Occasionally there's a single thump or a series of bumps, indicating some sort of floating deadhead or log rolling along under the tow.

I met Mark on the head of the tow, and he took out his papers and tobacco and rolled a smoke while I carefully checked the running lights. On the very head of the tow, you can hear the river water gurgling as it is pushed into a slight mound before it slips under and past down the sides of the barges. The smell of the river at night is especially sharp with the odor of various plants, algae, and microorganisms clinging to life in the muddy water. It is always the same for me—captivating.

"Yer gonna like workin' the Upper. Tows are almost always *built on both ends*. Only occasional pickin' up or droppin' and making locks on every watch."

"Wow. What a pleasure that will be to have a tow already built when you get to where you're going. Not like the Illinois River. You ever work over there? We were building tow on one end or the other every few days. I learned to enjoy that work, but it sure will be nice to have it done for us."

All this rigging was installed by fleet workers when they built the tow.

built on both ends - when tows are already built at each location (end) so the towboat can be immediately back underway

I could see Mark's several days' growth of beard in the light of his match as he relit his homemade cigarette. "Yeah, I worked over there some. That's why I stay over here. I always end up with a trip or two over there in the winter, but soon as it opens on the Upper in the spring I'm back here. Hate them damn old coal boats."

Mark was taller than me by a couple of inches and very slender. His life jacket looked far too big for him, and his clothes were dirty and torn. His body odor was pronounced and fascinating at the same time. A sharp slap-in-the-face of bittersweetness that took your breath away. Almost overwhelming. Yikes!

Upbound towboat passing Prescott, Wisconsin at mile marker 811.5

The night we passed Prescott for the first time came and went uneventfully. It was early morning, and I walked out onto the tow far enough to be entirely alone with my thoughts and away from the din of the boat. How peaceful my hometown looked at 4:00 a.m. Streetlights flickered, the two tall, historic, and easily identifiable steeples of the Catholic church were softly lit and dominant above the bluff. I had a peaceful backwards look at Main Street with all the storefronts facing away from the river onto the business district.

Sorta wished someone knew I was passing by, successful in my new career. No cell phones then. A long-distance phone call was no small undertaking in 1970, so letting anyone know I would be there was not happening.

I said a thoughtful, kind prayer thanking everyone who had helped me grow from a child to an adult in that lovely, kind river town. And I prayed an earnest thank-you for the fulfillment I felt that night in my new job.

This photo was taken as author was walking back
towards the towboat
from the head of this coal tow.

"Tell me a little about the friends you made and your new coworkers. Did that all go well?"

"Most of the people you work with on towboats are only in your life for a brief time. You or they might be midway through a hitch, so the folks you work with are constantly changing. Lots of interesting characters and lots of delightful stories."

Chapter 12
It's a Small World

"George, what can you tell me about the *Ida Crown*?"

"Struve! You want that job? She's a good boat. Smallest that Material Service runs, but they tell me she's good duty. Why don't ya try 'er? Right up here in Lockport. They want ya up there today."

So began my first hitch with Material Service. Their towboats operated on the Upper Illinois River, and most of the barges they towed had sand, rock, and materials mined locally that were in demand along the river and in Chicago. I accepted that job at the union hall before lunch and reported to their main shop and office not far away, near the famous Statesville Correctional Center, a maximum-security prison near Lockport, Illinois.

MV Northland downbound with gravel tow on the Illinois River.

Almost a mile down a limestone rock road I found a big two-tone Quonset hut, orange on the bottom and yellow on the top. This curved, ribbed, spartan metal building housed the mechanical shop and the dispatch offices for Material Service. Two of their towboats were moored against the limestone wall just inside from the main channel of the canal that passed by there. This mooring area also contained several sand and gravel ***deck barges*** in various states of repair.

The two boats were the MV *Ida Crown* and the MV *Alfred A.*

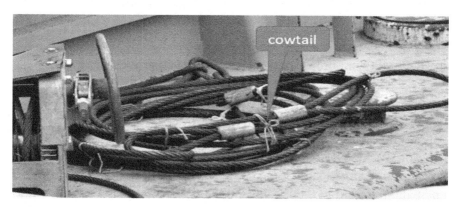

deck barges - same size as typical barges but the entire deck of the barge and the material ing transported are above the waterline

Hagerty. The MV *Ida Crown* appeared even smaller than it was, located next to the MV *Hagerty*. Both towboats were painted with the same orange-and-yellow scheme, the company colors. Each had a single deck with a telescopic pilothouse that enabled them to transit all the canals and the Upper Illinois River in nearby Chicago without needing to open any of the dozens of bridges there.

I was taking this all in while slowly walking down to the towboats with my bags. I approached the MV *Ida Crown* anxious to discover if I was in the right place.

"You here for the deck job?"

"Yep. Just came up from the hall in Joliet. I'm Tom Struve."

A very fit man with Coke-bottle glasses smiled broadly at me. He reached out and grabbed my hand, firmly and with enthusiasm. "Yer from Prescott, ain't ya! Yer old man is Bob Struve, right?" That greeting was followed by something that was a cross between a smile, a laugh, a cough, and a wheeze. "I'm Bobby Lubich. I'm the mate here." More grinning, sneezing, wheezing, grinning and not letting go of my hand. His effusive welcome was awkward but felt kinda good.

When he finally let go of me, he stepped back but kept smiling and staring at me, with his hands on his hips. Muscles bulging, a large knife in an easy-access holster, a flashlight in another, a *cowtail* in one back pocket, and a second set of leather work gloves in the other. He looked the part of the consummate towboat deck professional.

I racked my brain trying to think of how I might know my new crew boss. There were bunches of Lubichs in Prescott. My family rented a broken-down, nasty old house from a Joe Lubich when we first moved into town from the farm.

"Not sure we've met before, but I'm glad to be here. My first time on a Material Service boat."

cowtail - single strand from a large line used on the river like twine and used to keep lines and wires coiled for easy storage, transporting, and organization

MV *Ida Crown* alongside sand and gravel barges, her most frequent cargo.

"I'll look after you. You new on the river?"

"I've been working on Valley Line boats outta the hall since May. The *Heekin* here on the canal, and the *Thompson, Dresden, Central*, and *Brandon* on the coal run back and forth to Havana. Even got a trip over on the Upper on the *WS Rhea*. Really enjoying this. All I ever wanted to do."

"I'll show you yer room and introduce you to the cook so you kin git yer linens."

I lugged my gear aft, and Bob pointed to a door that was open on a tiny room with two beds and a small locker. The bottom bunk was vacant, so that would be my first lower bunk on a towboat to date. The room smelled musty, and I felt a strong urge to wipe down all the surfaces and clean the floor. I would get to that later.

"How'd you git this old tub?"

"Came out of the hall in Joliet. Just happened to stop by on my way home and saw this. Been wantin' to get on with Material Service to see how it goes with them."

The cook, Jim Owens, was a pale, trim fellow with a number of silver hairs here and there. Snow-white goatee and mustache, twinkling blue eyes, with a smile that made you feel comfortable immediately. The galley was super compact. Clean and smelled fantastic, but smaller by far than the kitchen facilities on the boats I'd worked recently. Jim gave me my linens and told me to be sure not to miss his award-winning chili, grits, and pot roast that were the day's lunch offerings. *What a nice guy.*

I was storing my gear when my bunkmate came in.

"I'm Jimmy. Jimmy Sugrannis. **Got 22 days today**. Gittin' off to-morrow or the next day, so I give ya the bottom bunk."

"Thanks a ton. So, how does it go with this little tiny boat? I'm just starting out, and this is the smallest boat I've been on."

"'Cept fer these small rooms, she's okay. Good duty. Two or three barges up the north side mostly. She's only seven hundred fifty horsepower. The river is small up there, and still we barely fit in lotta places. Everybody's real friendly. Gotta be win yer right on top a each other like this. Once in a while we git a trip to the south side, but not too much. Jist back 'n forth, back 'n forth. I been a regular here for two years. Like it way better'n Valley Line. Them boats is *hard* work!"

Material Service tow of sand on the canal at Romeoville, Illinois

got twenty-two days today - commonplace for crews to discuss the number of days since get-ting aboard the towboat

"It'll be fun to try this out. I've seen some Material Service jobs go out of the hall but never had seniority enough to get one. Must be a good company. Twenty-one-day hitches, huh? Do you like that?"

"Oh yeah. Got a super frisky girlfriend over in Pekin, and I can't wait to get back in her arms. Three weeks is all I can stand to be away!"

"Nice to meet you. I better get up forward and get ready to work. Thanks again for givin' me the bottom bunk."

Once more, I scoped out the least filthy and newest-looking life jacket from those hanging in the forward deck locker. Hardly room to turn around, but everything was tidy and in its place. The *Ida Crown* slid back to the stern of the single string of barges, and the captain maneuvered the nimble boat up against the barge loaded with sand.

In the modest pilothouse, I could see a smiling face. "Turn her loose, Bobby," the captain said over the speaker. =

Center "bits" on the head deck of a towboat. This is a safety line attached to the barge.

I wrapped a *safety line* between the center kevel of the barge

safety line - a line fastened between the bits on the head deck and the center fitting on the barge directly forward as a safety precaution in case a face wire breaks

and *the bits* on the head deck of the towboat and grabbed a cheater bar and toothpicks to head out and check the tow. I followed Bob, my new boss, down the side of the single string of barges. That was new. When you have barges two or more wide in a tow, you mostly walk back and forth between the two strings. On a single string, you need to be more careful because the river is just inches below and alongside you.

Arriving at the steering coupling, I inserted my toothpicks and started to tighten ratchets. My new mentor gave me a wide grin. Apparently, my understanding of what needed to be done and getting out there and doing it made him happy. After I got both original sets of fore and aft wires tight, he and I jerked tight the *double-ups* he had laid out.

The double-up sets of rigging are installed as a security measure to give an additional level of safety to the coupling where it is warranted.

"We're gonna do everything extra safe! I like lotsa riggin'. Can't be too careful!"

Bobby Lubich wasn't a big talker. Occasional discussions about what to do and how it should be done and that was pretty much it. I tried to make casual conversation occasionally and eventually gave up. He had a job to do, and a lot of visiting was not included in that formula.

I learned a lot on that trip. Bobby went far out of his way to show me everything that was different about working towboats handling sand and gravel barges into and out of Chicago. Material Service operated major limestone quarries near their home office in Lockport. Most of the raw materials we shipped into the city aboard their barges eventually became concrete.

The MV *Ida Crown* was very modest, but she was a tough old

the bits - pair of oversized timberheads located on the head deck of a towboat
double-ups - additional set of rigging installed over the original set for extra measure of safety

gal. The upper reaches of the Illinois River terminate several nautical miles downstream from downtown Chicago. Bridges are everywhere. Beginning at Joliet, massive railroad lift spans and many bascule bridges open regularly for all types of river and towboat traffic. Farther upstream, beginning at Lemont, Illinois, most of the bridges have not opened since the 1940's when wartime shipbuilding was underway. The MV *Ida Crown*, like all towboats that operate upstream from Lemont, has a telescopic pilothouse. The captain would keep it as high as possible traveling along and at the last minute would lower it just enough to squeeze under the many bridges.

As was the custom on all towboats, fresh, hot coffee was delivered to the pilothouse periodically during a watch. Each captain had unique desires, it seemed, and instructions for how to make the coffee varied.

Another Material Service towboat pushing two loads and two empty deck barges

"It's gotta be fresh. Don't bring me nothin' but fresh. About half a cup a grounds in the *drip strainer* for me, and make sure the water run through it is boilin' when you pour it into the top." Captain Jimmy Connors was very particular. "I want my first cup at one p.m. and one a.m. at night. A second cup at three in the afternoon. Heat the cup up a little too with some hot water."

"Got it. So, you worked for these guys long?"

Jimmy was short and round. He wasn't so much heavy as he was thick. He had a friendly smile, and he loved to visit. We chatted about everything, and it was clear he enjoyed my visits to the pint-sized pilothouse. He especially enjoyed discussing his family and Illinois history.

"My twelfth year with 'em. My kids are gone, so just me and the old lady. She comes in 'bout midway through a trip and stays for a day or so, and that makes it nice. Only an hour from here to the house. These three-week trips is lots better'n the thirty-day hitches everybody else runs. You gonna make a career out here?"

"It sure looks like it. All I ever wanted to do. I got river in my blood. Can't beat the time off and the working conditions, I think. I really enjoy all the traveling, and I love the great cooks and food."

Bobby seldom came up to the pilothouse. He lit one cigarette off the last and spent a lot of time milling around, quietly watching life on the riverbank as we passed. One afternoon as we laid by at the shop for repairs, he introduced me to some new swear words and a fid.

A fid is a wooden tool shaped like the barrel of a baseball bat that comes to a point. Barges are moored to the bank and sometimes to each other with thick ropes called "lines," and a fid is called for when

drip strainer – coffee pot having a top section into which boiling water was poured, which then dripped slowly through the basket of grounds to create fresh, hot coffee

you need to *splice* two lines into one or to make an *eye* at the end of a line.

You insert the pointed end of the fid into the weave of the line to separate the strands (usually three strands).

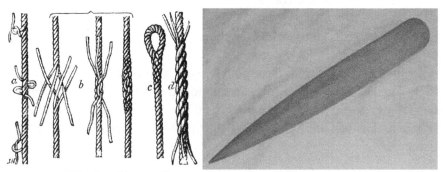

Wooden fid as well as common splices created using a fid.

"I don't understand why these cheap bastards can't get some nice poly lines like everybody else!"

We had just taken the bindings off a 600-foot coil of three-inch *African sisal line*. We measured and cut the line into fifteen forty-foot lengths and began splicing an eye that was about three feet wide into one end of each of the new mooring lines. Bobby was not fond of just sitting around and relaxing, so this was our task for that nice summer afternoon. With a great deal of grunting and hammering of that wooden fid into the stiff, unyielding sisal rope, we eventually swore and fought our way through all fifteen, tying the last one up in a coil with a cowtail and stowing them below the head deck in the line locker.

"I hate that no-good, daguuum junk! I don't know why we gotta use that. 'Bout kills a man gittin' it ready and ain't worth a damn to use neither!"

splice - process of weaving marine ropes into each other or weaving an eye into a line
eye - circular loop at the end of most mooring lines used in marine work
African sisal line - organic, questionable quality, undesirable, super inexpensive, thick, very stiff rope used mostly for mooring barges   "I

Those were probably the most pleasant comments Bobby uttered in frustration that afternoon. I found the exercise of splicing the eye into each line kind of interesting—a new challenge—but most everything was new and fun for me.

Bobby came to the end of his trip a few days later. I bid him farewell and thanked him profusely for all the special attention he had showered upon me.

"You git back on here, and me and you, we make a good team! Talk to these guys. They will git you here regular."

I assured him that I would look into it. I wasn't sure it was that simple, but he seemed convinced that we could arrange to work together in the future. I did learn a lot from him, and the *Ida Crown* was a lovely towboat.

A man nicknamed "Wahoo" replaced Bobby. Never heard him referred to by his real name. He was another taciturn man. No one discussed his Native American heritage, and he didn't make anything of it either. He was the second mate, and I did what he told me to do.

Wahoo had this amazing physique, and he never wore a shirt. Incredibly toned chest and cut six-pack abs. A strikingly handsome man, chiseled jaw, thick black hair pulled back. The whole deal. Shortest denim cutoffs I had ever seen on a human.

On our trips into the north side during daylight hours (the northern leg of the Sanitary and Ship Canal that flowed south from downtown Chicago) Wahoo would be sure to situate himself out on the bow of the sand or gravel barge we were delivering to the Material Service shoreside dock at West Chicago Avenue just under the Halsted Street bridge. Immediately downstream from that bridge on the right bank going upstream was the multistory Montgomery Ward mail order fulfillment center.

Montgomery Ward's fulfillment center in the 1970's
along the bank of the Chicago River.

One set of windows vertically aligned on that building turned out to be women's restrooms. Each time we passed, Wahoo quite willingly, and me not so much, would get pelted with all manner of objects, most containing phone numbers tossed from those windows. I found it incredible. Wahoo seemed to enjoy it.

When my three weeks had passed, I put in for relief. I got off the *Ida Crown* a couple days later, happy for the experience and hoping I would see her again. As George, the union boss had said, she was a good boat, good duty.

"Tell me a little about the folks who work on towboats."

"Most river workers at that time were relatively unsophisticated and uneducated. People unafraid of demanding work, they all took pride in being self-sufficient and independent. Mostly conservative, loving, and willing to help one another without question. Folks filled with character and joy."

Chapter 13
Skeeter Liked Me and I Liked Him

"Tommy, this isn't a job, it's a *position!*"

Captain Skeeter Ranson was holding court as we were towboating up the *south side* early one evening in November heading for the South Chicago Harbor. Skeeter had been with the company many years, so he was almost always captain aboard this company's towboats.

The pilot on the front watch was always the captain (6:00 a.m. to noon and 6:00 p.m. to midnight). The pilot on the after watch (noon to 6:00 p.m. and midnight to 6:00 a.m.) was simply known as the "pilot" and was subordinate to the captain. Captains' duties were pretty much what you'd expect. The captain is the CEO of the boat, making final decisions and in charge of administrative, personnel, and financial matters concerning the everyday operation of the vessel.

south side - common term for navigating upbound into Chicago having selected to go to the south side of city via the SAG Canal

I had gone up to the pilothouse to bring Skeeter his 7:00 p.m. coffee. He liked a fresh cup brewed in an old-fashioned drip pot, and he loved it when you brought it to him hot, right after it finished dripping.

We were on board the MV *Viking*, a **triple-screw**, telescopic pilothouse boat moving slowly along upstream with four barges **strung out** in a row. It was cold outside, and the modest milkhouse electric heater only intensified the odors of the river tracked in on the pilothouse floor.

MV *Viking*, 1,200-hp, three-engine towboat with telescopic pilothouse.

I was assigned to boats that Skeeter captained many times and really enjoyed being on his watch. He was a true storyteller who loved to visit and share his often confrontational and/or provoking perspectives. He liked to rail about injustices and loved getting a rise out of people. I was welcome in his pilothouse during periods of inactivity when we navigated from one place to another, and I learned a great deal about towboating—and life—from Skeeter.

"Here you go, Captain," I said as I slid the cup in among the assorted items on the captain's console. I cleared a space near the three

triple screw - The word "screw" means "propeller" in the marine world. If a towboat has one engine and propeller it is called single screw. Two drivetrains: twin screw. Three: triple screw.
strung out - a tow of barges that is a single string (one barge wide) fastened together end to end

Westinghouse air-pneumatic *ship ups* and midway between the two sets of levers that were the steering and backing rudder sticks. A pair of 3x50 binoculars were right nearby, resting on a thick terry cloth towel.

Photo of two *ship ups* on towboat console of a twin screw towboat.

"You make damn good coffee, Tommy."

As discussed previously, towboat coffee possesses a unique coffee brewing technique. A plain metal coffee pot with a drip brewing container at the top with tiny holes where the boiling water seeps down through the coffee below but above the pot. Really tasty because it is very fresh, and how much coffee is used determines how strong it is. Each towboat pilothouse professional has a specific time or (times) they want it brewed and delivered and very particular requirements about how strong it should be.

"Thanks, Captain."

"How many days you got this trip, Tommy?"

ship ups - On the captain's console, these levers are connected to the towboat's engines. Straight up, the levers indicate neutral. Moving forward the engine power increases accordingly. Same with reverse and moving the levers (or ship ups) backward.

"Twenty-one including today."

"Jeez. You're getting close!"

"Yup! Probably gonna get off right at my thirty days this time. The girlfriend and I are gonna go to Key West with the camper."

Like so many Illinois rivermen, Skeeter spoke with a slang that would have been much more at home in the Deep South. He would draw words out for maximum impact and favored that informal Southern style of speaking with little concern for the value of enunciation. Sometimes when he spoke, I could see him in the courtroom as a quasi-sophisticated gentleman lawyer with a fine suit and a bow tie, slowly stating his closing argument before a jury about to consider sending someone to death row. He often e-nun-ci-a-ted and exhibited facial expressions far more dramatic than necessary for the small talk we were making.

He would say, "Tom"—drawing out my name into three or more syllables—"what do you think about the way the government is handling our money?"

Without waiting for me to respond, he would tell me what he thought.

"I'll tell you this. It's a damn shame how everything has grown out of control. The business owners in the small town I come from are always telling me about how the government makes them do this and then that. And they can't get ahead. No sir, they just keep struggling along. And it ain't right, I tell you! Do you know there's talk that a Walmart might be going in that little damn town that I come from, and do you know, that will be it. That'll be the death knell for all the little homegrown businesses. We already got a Kmart and a Pamida, and when they came, we'd liked to all have given up!"

His unusually left-leaning remarks about politics and life in general provided a superior insight into Southern men and especially

Southern rivermen even though Skeeter lived only as far south as Central Illinois. Those men had strong opinions, staunch conservative views, and gentlemanly manners. They respected and revered God, country, the law, and working hard to make something of themselves. They had no time for freeloaders and spoke frequently about people of character and their accomplishments, victories, and joys.

MV Kiowa, sister towboat to MV *Viking*, both with telescopic pilothouses.
Shown here on Illinois River in Joliet, Illinois.

These rivermen had a single-minded respect for the town or city they came from. In fact, in Illinois at that time, it was common for men to have their name and hometown custom painted on both doors of their pickups.

Skeeter was from Morris, Illinois. He shared terrific and almost worshipful details about his family, extended family, his hometown and hometown values, and the key issues there. He adored that Midwest respect for community and the reverence and esteem folks have for their heritage and history. People did business with a handshake, and your promise was your word. Local community ties were important, and folks loved hard, played hard, and worked hard. Americana at its finest.

When Skeeter declared he had not a job but a position, he was commenting in his own modest way that he was thrilled to have come that far in an otherwise unassuming life. To have achieved the status in his hometown of being called Captain Ransom was an outstanding accomplishment.

In many ways Captain Skeeter and others like him affirmed my decision to become a riverman when many kids my age went on to college after high school. I was free, wildly successful, and working when and how much I wanted. Because I had learned respect, manners, and a little charm along the way as a youngster, I was welcomed and accepted easily in every marine work setting. I traveled all over the country living a remarkable journeyman's life and had lots of unconventional time off, so I could hunt for extended periods in the fall and snowmobile for days at a time in the winter, two of my passions at the time.

My invaluable early life learning about how to get along and work hard as part of a team was reinforced among these men of strong and significant character. The work was hard physical labor—not for everyone—in the rain and the heat and the cold. We were away from home and our loved ones, and we didn't complain or feel sorry for ourselves. All of us were rewarded with independence, and our individual successes were well deserved and hard earned.

Skeeter liked me and I liked him. He and so many others just like him taught me the art of a delightful story and maybe even the art of a modest fib woven in. After all, what remarkable story has not been embellished over time and with each telling?

To this day, I can see him swinging around in that captain's chair as I came through the pilothouse door. His ample girth spilled over a little bit, but that generous, gregarious smile below the overgrown eyebrows and twinkling eyes always welcomed a fellow traveler on the road of life to a little visit to make the time go by.

"was it cold in the winter? Did the river freeze over? was it difficult working in freezing conditions?"

"I remember that first winter as being really cold. Ice was everywhere, and I sensed that it was not always that way. Many veteran towboaters said that was the most brutal winter they had experienced. It was imperative that we not let a line get wet. It would freeze stiff as a tree limb and was of no use after that."

Chapter 14
Fire!

"Fire! Fire! Fire!" I yelled as I burst into the galley on board the towboat MV *Manco*.

We were working the south Chicago River just downstream from the historic steel mills that had once made Chicago an awesome industrial giant. It was midwinter about 1971, and thanks to heavy ice, we couldn't navigate the Acme Steel bend, a very sharp, tight turn along the Calumet-Sag Channel on the way upstream into south Chicago. The ice makes it impossible to traverse the sharp turn and pass into and through the bridge there with three barges strung out.

So before we could continue, we had to break up the ice immediately south of the narrow bridge at the upstream end of the bend. In order to do that, we **knocked out** the towboat and made several passes upstream and down loosening the grip the ice had on the tow. Navigating without a tow is called being **light boat**. We followed a zigzag pattern attempting to break up about twelve inches of ice, the result of the most recent cold spell. Any boat moving up or downstream there has the same task when the channel is clogged with ice.

The bumping and grinding of breaking up the ice had caused a small, portable electric heater in the starboard aft stateroom opposite mine to fall off a chair and set the bedding on fire. I smelled smoke in my room and a feeling of dread came over me. I crossed the hall and opened the door to the other cabin. The heater was leaning against the blankets, and there was a very small fire. I slammed the door shut and raced forward down the hall in four or five long strides, banging on the doors of my boatmates, then leaped across the threshold into the galley.

The MV *Manco* was a beautiful historic towboat.
Single-screw, 1,150-hp direct-air-reversible Morse-Duesenberg engine.

knocked out - when the crew removes the cables that attach the towboat to the barges
light boat - a towboat that is maneuvering without barges

AJ, the boat's *chief engineer*, was talking to the cook, and they both jumped out of their chairs.

AJ had a most unusual face. In most ways he was a normal-looking man with a wonderful smile, but something had gone wrong with his nose. It was very large and decorated with a cacophony of colors—blue, green, deep purple—as well as a handful of wartlike growths. Once you caught sight of it, it was like a car wreck; you couldn't look away.

I saw real fear in his eyes, mostly because this boat was attached to him and him to her. The old towboat *Manco* was from another time. A single-screw, 1,150-horsepower, lovely old vessel with a Morse Duesenberg *direct-air-reversible* engine. For those wondering why that is significant, picture a massive diesel engine thirty feet from front to back, four feet wide, and twelve feet high, with twelve cylinders each about twenty-four inches in diameter. That engine was from an era when sophisticated technology was still a dream.

Operation of that engine, approximately fifty years after it was built, required full-time love and attention, unlike more-recent modern diesel engines. So AJ had a relatively secure job in a time when some towboat engineering jobs weren't. He knew that towboat backwards and forwards and upside down, and as long as that boat kept running, he was an invaluable resource necessary for its operation and was, for all intents and purposes, irreplaceable.

We raced back down the hall towards the stern. Together, we opened that door again, and alarming flames burst out at us. The oxygen we'd let into that room was all that was needed to turn the small fire into a raging blaze, consuming every combustible in the cabin. We

Chief Engineer - a specially trained person responsible for repairing and maintaining all the equipment and systems on a towboat
direct air reversible - Unlike modern diesel engines that run continuously, this antique engine was connected directly to the propeller shaft, and it was either turning the propeller forward or in reverse. When the engine was in neutral it was stopped.

had a genuine catastrophe on our hands, so I pulled the ***general alarm button*** on our way forward. Towboats are made of steel, so the fire stayed, for a time, relatively contained. The interior finishes and bunks were on fire, and even though the conflagration was confined to the stern area and stateroom quarters, an inferno around tanks of fuel and oily equipment is very dangerous.

Sensing the gravity of the situation, the pilot left our barges mired in the ice and pushed the boat into the bank at a spot where we could all get off.

MV *Manco* pushed against bank in the ice on Illinois River.

I remember the fear on the face of our cook, Tom Cullen. He was anxious about climbing up the tow knee steps rising from the deck because it was three- to four-foot jump from the top of the tow knee onto the riverbank. Likewise, it was about a four-foot climb up to the head deck and that was not possible either. Tom weighed in at nearly 400 pounds, so his mobility was severely limited. He finally and reluctantly climbed the steps and stood at the top of the tow knee. We discussed the possibilities.

general alarm button - Every towboat has numerous fixtures with a switch to enable the general alarm. A very loud continuously ringing bell alerts the entire crew to an emergency.

"I'm never gonna make it, Tom."

"You have to get off. Don't worry, I'll catch you."

When he finally stopped glancing back at the black smoke rising from the stern of the boat, he did jump. It was like watching a water balloon contract and expand when he tumbled and rolled out onto the frozen ground.

You could see genuine relief in his anxious smile, now in a safe place and with no obvious injuries. With the boat pressed against the bank, the entire crew was on land close by and afraid of an explosion or who knows what as the fire continued to spread.

The entire crew, except AJ. He remained on the boat alone, certain he could save her. He proceeded quickly through the mechanics of hooking up the fire hose and starting a fire pump going. After much ado (it was freezing outside, so the fittings and the hose did not function at first because they were all frozen) he got enough water going to extinguish the fire after about fifteen minutes. He had to deal with lots of noxious fumes and some serious risk, but he was determined. AJ and that boat had been together a long, long time, so his emotional connection was doubtless significant. We were all in awe of his single-minded tenacity and his bravery during the fire.

Another of that company's boats was dispatched to gather up the abandoned (and frozen in place) barges and the wounded *Manco* and bring them back to headquarters. After spending a night at a hotel, those of us who'd lost personal belongings were taken out the next day to buy and replace everything we had on the boat.

"You had *how many* pairs of shoes on board?" our port captain, Lowell Bailey, asked me.

Because I traveled all over the country in my RV/camper van in between assignments on towboats, I had virtually all my personal belongings with me always.

"Lowell, I am thrilled to be able to replace my tired old clothes that went up in smoke. I am very grateful to Twin City Barge."

Lowell replied, "We are just all very happy that no one was injured, and everyone got off the boat safely. It is a very small thing to help replace your personal things, and the company is happy to do it."

Authors photo of the starboard walkway looking forward on the *Manco*. We are pushing a string of loaded barges upbound on the SAG Canal heading for South Chicago Harbor.

"Did working as a deckhand help you learn about piloting tow-boats?"

"Absolutely. Like any internship or entry-level job, the work on the decks of the barges and towboats is critical to understanding how it all works. I was especially keen on watching every captain I could perform all the tasks associated with piloting. I asked lots of questions, and captains would occasionally let me steer for them."

Chapter 15
You Better Take It, Larry

I was steering for Captain Larry Hetrick aboard the MV *Pawnee* in the spring of 1973. Twin City Barge fostered an environment enabling towboat crews to advance in their jobs. If a deck professional wanted to become a pilot, they would issue a *steering letter* on behalf of that person. The steering letter gave the pilot at the helm a level of comfort that the company would be understanding if an accident happened while the student pilot was steering in lieu of the pilot on watch.

steering letter - authorization from the towboat company for select deck crew members to operate the towboat under the watchful eye of the pilot on watch as part of their training.

Larry was unique in his willingness to let a deckhand *really* steer while he was on watch. Everything, not just the easy stuff. He would sit back on the couch in the pilothouse and either doze or read or visit with you. Every other pilot or captain who let me steer for him only did so when we were traveling along in some safe stretch of river where virtually nothing could go wrong.

The *Pawnee* was a 1,000-horsepower towboat operated by Twin City Barge. She was a modest vessel, and the telescopic pilothouse was considerably lower than some at full extension. Larry was the pilot, working the after watch—noon to 6:00 p.m. and midnight to 6:00 a.m. I was the lead deckhand on the forward watch, so I could steer for him during his afternoon watch when I would otherwise have been resting.

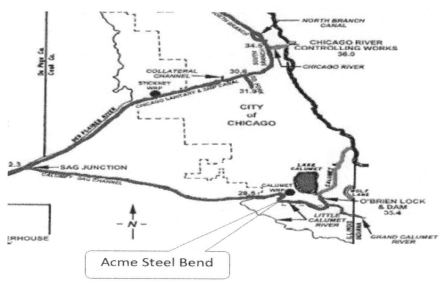

Acme Steel Bend

We were headed upstream on a brisk February afternoon, approaching the Acme Steel Bend (the same difficult stretch of river where the MV *Manco* caught fire, as I talked about in Chapter 14). The Acme Steel Company had a mammoth steel manufacturing facility there that was no longer viable, but the huge buildings and infrastructure loomed over a ***horseshoe bend*** in the river.

horseshoe bend - a bend in the river shaped like a horseshoe—changing course almost 180 degrees

At the very upstream corner of that sharp bend, a narrow, nasty old railroad bridge crossed the river. We had four empty barges strung out in a line, and as we approached the bend, the wind was strong from the side. The tow was sliding despite my *hard down* steering, and it seemed like the turning of the tow had stalled.

"You better take it, Larry."

"Whaddaya mean? You're doin' fine."

"No, I'm serious. This doesn't look very good. She's sliding, and I ain't gonna make this steer. We're gonna crash."

Larry got up off the couch, stood a minute assessing the situation, and sat back down. "I'll tell you what, stud. I'll take it if you really want me to. But if I do, you just head your little fat ass down those stairs and don't ever come up here and ask me to steer again. Yer either gonna do this or you ain't. You make up your mind."

He stuck his face back in his magazine. I took that to mean he was not alarmed. Eventually the head of the tow did start to come back around, and I pulled back the throttles, letting our headway run out. Very near the bridge the river narrowed, so the wind had less effect. I was pleased as I carefully watched my headway against the nearby bank. With only seventy horizontal feet in which to insert our thirty-five-foot-wide string of barges, I breathed a quiet, private sigh when the deckhand on the head waved *all clear* as the bow of the tow entered under the bridge 820 feet forward from me.

I was especially interested in steering every minute I could because I had an appointment in two short weeks at the Coast Guard office in Chicago to take my towboat captain license exam. Larry was a great mentor. Mostly he would only respond to my questions, and he let me

hard down - when the captain has the steering levers all the way in one direction; steering as hard as you can in one direction
all clear - a deckhand will wave one extended arm up and down indicating the head of the tow is past the point of concern

get myself into and out of the same kinds of difficult situations any pilot or captain might experience. During those long times in between the *tight spots*, we enjoyed visiting. Larry loved a story, and he laughed unabashedly.

There was a lighthearted, childlike innocence to all his observations and wisdom. He was on this earth to have fun and made no bones about it. There was no end to the tales he told about growing up in rural Minnesota and all his adventures as he grew into manhood.

Robert Street Highway Bridge in downtown St. Paul.
Cothart's motorcycle ride occurred over the top of those arches.

"You shoulda seen the time that Red Cothart rode his motorcycle right up over those side arches on the Robert Street Highway Bridge. I wouldn'ta believed it if I hadn't seen it. That crazy sonofabitch flew his plane underneath the railroad and the Robert Street Highway bridge right there too! He had some hairy experiences in Nam, and he ain't scared of nothin' now."

Soon to pass my third anniversary as a deck professional, I had a few remarkable stories to share also.

tight spot - anywhere where the channel closes in or maneuvering becomes challenging because of lack of room

"Did you have to go in the draft lottery, Larry?"

"Me and Cothart went down to sign up together, but they wouldn't take me. I had rheumatic fever when I was a kid, and that knocked me out. I'da known that, I wouldn'ta told 'em!"

"Last August when they held the Vietnam lottery drawing," I told him, "I was on the *Ida Crown* in Chicago. Little, dinky-ass black-and-white TV that barely worked. Tinfoil on the antenna—you know that deal. The guy announced my birthday, and right then we went under a bridge and the TV lost reception! I was so pissed! The guys had such a big laugh. I didn't see much humor in it. Had to wait till the next day till I could get a paper from the lockman at O'Brien Lock to find out what my number was. Didn't end up havin' to go."

"I'da gone over. We didn't have nothin' better to do! I got tossed outta high school, and I was ready for anything with a purpose!" Larry sounded genuinely annoyed all those years later.

"Did you ever do winter towing, Larry? It's so damn cold up there right now, it's incredible. I haven't done any this winter, but last year I made a couple of short trips on the *Viking* there with Denny Schickling. Man, I never was so cold! Ice was two, three feet thick. So thick that we almost couldn't break through it with just the towboat. The tow-boat's owners made us lay by at the loading terminal with the barge while it was loading so we had always had the weight of the barge out in front of the boat to break ice."

I can't begin to describe the abuse that towboat endured crashing over and over through ice up to three or four feet thick. The contract moving that oil barge under those brutal conditions must have been very profitable to offset the cost of the damage to the towboat.

"That ice just beats those poor boats to pieces. We put her on the dry dock at State Street, and two of the three propellers were missing an entire *fluke*, and all three had bent flukes. You couldn't hardly keep

fluke - slang for propeller blade

anything on the counter in the galley. That boat shook like nothing I had ever seen."

Photo of barge being pushed through heavy ice.

Larry nodded, and I could tell he knew exactly what I was talking about.

"You know Buddy Bilderback, right?" I said next. "D'you ever eat his cookin'? Man, he can really cook.

He made us a new soup every day that last trip. He is such a serious old fart. I call him Builder Buddyback. That'd get a smile outta him every time."

Larry chuckled, and his generous belly jiggled where it hung over his belt. He said, "No cook on there? How the hell did they git away with that? You guys got day-for-day though, right?"

"I don't know how we got by without a cook. They bought us groceries though. Yeah, and we got day-for-day," I continued. "Musta been some kinda deal that Denny worked out with the company. Old Captain Denny really earned his money though. Me'n Buddy could sleep some off and on back and forth, but whenever a barge was ready, we had to go. I think he was putting in more than twelve hours a day.

Man! It is the coldest work I ever did." I just about shivered only thinking about it.

"We pretty much just slept in our clothes, Larry. The little heaters in those rooms couldn't keep up. I woke up one day with my hair frozen to the wall. We'd have to knock out the boat and break ice and try to get the barge close to the dock. Then knock the boat out again and break some more ice! Dang, it was cold! Glad I'm down here this winter!"

"I'm glad you're here too, stud! It's been a gravy train for me with you steerin' every afternoon." Larry let out another of his great laughs. He was such a fun guy to be around. "I hope I'm still on here when we take this old tub back around. I've done that every spring for the past couple'a years, and it's really a fun trip."

Larry was talking about taking the MV *Pawnee* down the Illinois River to meet the Mississippi near St. Louis and then heading north to eventually return to St. Paul, Twin City Barge's home port and head-quarters.

"I love workin' up there in the spring *when the water gits up*. Whistling out of the Minnesota River with them downbound grain tows gives me a kick! Wasn't you up there when they knocked the pilothouse off the *Santee* last spring?" Larry asked, laughing.

"You bet I was. I was knocked out of bed into about three inches of water on the floor. When she hit the very end of the swing bridge, the pilothouse folded backwards, and that pushed the forward section of the towboat down enough that we had water on the floor of the for-ward deck room where I was sleeping."

"Carl Bales. Man!" Larry chimed in. "He never turned on the gen-eral alarm or anything. That poor bastard. He used to *ride the entire summer*, and then he was drunk, I think, all winter back in Illinois

when the water gits up - anytime the river rises, flood stage, for example
ride the entire summer - occasionally towboat workers would get aboard a towboat in early spring and not get off until late fall

145

Old Cedar Avenue Highway Bridge across the Minnesota River
struck by our towboat, the MV *Santee*.

where he came from. I worked with him a couple of times in the spring
when he came back. Brutal! You talk about sick? Man!"

"So anyway, when I came out on the deck and started upstairs on
the *Santee*, I could see the bridge kind of swaying after the collision. I
thought it might topple into the river. The tow we were pushing was
two loaded barges strung out.

On the downstream end of the two barges they had the MV *Sioux*
faced up. We were taking her to the dry dock in St. Paul. Skeeter had
run her backwards up onto a point there at Cargill and bent the steering
rudders.

"So there's poor old Carl. He's got the flagship towboat of the
company, the *Sioux*, on the head of the tow, and he can't stop above the
bridge. Too much current. This was when the turn-of-the-century Cedar
Avenue Bridge took forever to open. The current was cookin', and Carl
came grudgingly down above the bridge, praying it would be open in
time. The workers at that time twisted a long handle device manually
in a circle to turn the bridge on its turntable.

"Now, the bridge is not open all the way. We can't stop, so old Carl gets the *Sioux* and the bow of the two loads down into the bridge still backing all reverse but losing the fight against the fierce spring runoff current. He's got her flankin' for all he's worth, but *she won't lift her ass back up*. And *crunch*. Right smack into the end of the partially opened bridge the pilothouse of our towboat goes.

The author talking on the radio as a young steersman aboard the MV *Pawnee*

"It was the damnedest thing, Larry. The pilothouse just kinda laid back towards the stern. Apparently, Carl got down on the floor under

she won't lift her ass back up - When backing a towboat against a strong current, sometimes the current against the stern prevents the pilot from steering the boat where it needs to go.

the console, and it was strong enough to save him from being squished flat. I chopped enough steel away with a fire axe so we could drag him outta there. Know what the first thing he said was? 'Anybody got somethin' to drink?' Ha! Man! He was shook up! They fired up the *Sioux* and got us pushed over to the bank. I was so glad nobody got hurt."

Even though Larry already knew most of the story, he rewarded me with one of his great belly laughs.

"It is so great of you to let me steer all these days, Larry. Man, I am learning so much. I feel a lot more confident now. Nobody else lets guys like me actually do anything. They all just let you steer on some long, straight, boring stretch, and you really don't learn anything.

"I been studying like crazy for that test. I wish I knew how hard it was."

"Yer gonna do okay. Yer a natural. Everything you do is just like I would do it. It ain't rocket science. I've had fun visiting with you, too. It's all good!

"Good luck with your license. I never got one. They just turned me loose one day over at Minnesota Harbor Service, and I never looked back. Crazy bastards over there, them people. I was sure glad to git on here regular. Lots better boats and lots more work."

"So, you worked enough days and years to qualify to take the captain's test. Was that a hard test?"

"Yes, very hard. I selected the SAG Canal on the upper end of the Illinois for the river segment that would be the focus of the exam. The officer at the Chicago Coast Guard office made sure to emphasize the difficulty of the examination. I had studied hard and couldn't wait for the opportunity."

Chapter 16
Struve! Can You Cook?

I arrived at the twenty-first floor of the office building housing the Chicago Coast Guard headquarters a few minutes before my appointment. Everything looked like what you'd expect in a U.S. military setting. Spartan, threadbare furniture, no pictures, no paint. Service folks in Coast Guard uniforms sporting name tags and insignia noting their respective ranks.

I was greeted by young man who offered me coffee and a chair in the waiting area. After some time, a uniformed man who walked with the confidence of an officer approached me. I stood, we shook hands, and he introduced himself as Petty Officer Mark. He escorted me into a large, bright room with a huge desk surrounded by a handful of chairs. I found it hard not to look out the window to get a view of downtown Chicago from that height.

I passed a manila file to him containing all of the completed forms that had been sent to me. He looked at every page and then requested my driver's license and any second form of ID. Returning to the room, he brought with him a twenty-four-inch-high old-fashioned entry ledger. He took a seat next to me and opened it to the pages with the most recent entries. Each line had a person's name and farther over on the right-hand column of the page was the word "PASS" or "FAIL." I looked carefully, and I could only find a couple of "PASS" entries on the two pages I could see.

"I just want you to know how difficult this exam is. Not many people pass the first time. Just want to be up-front, so there are no surprises."

Department of
Homeland Security
United States
Coast Guard

Navigation Rules and Regulations Handbook

Containing – International and Inland Rules of the Road
and their respective Annexes
– Bridge-to-Bridge Radiotelephone Regulations
– Vessel Traffic Management Regulations
– Other pertinent regulations for waterway users

Petty Officer Mark went on to explain the process and the time frames. I ended up using all of the allowed six-hour time slots during the next two days just drawing the SAG canal upstream from Lockport Lock. It had to be all from memory, and every detail needed to be recorded: dozens of bridges, their dimensions, overhead lines and outfalls, depth of water everywhere, and nearly endless additional details.

On the third and final day, I took the written exam. The test questions covered the "Rules of the Road," all manner of marine construction, firefighting, first aid, and communication between vessels. There were hundreds of questions, and at the end of the exam I checked and rechecked and handed it in.

Petty Officer Mark left and returned about an hour later with the corrected exam. "I am sorry to tell you that you didn't make it. You did great on the mapping section of the exam. You passed all of the remaining sections except for the 'Rules of the Road.' So, the good news is you only have to retake that section. You have to wait thirty days, but once we get a passing grade on that piece, we will get you your license."

I was relieved and a little disappointed but that much more determined to make it happen. I would study for that section all over again to be prepared for the retest. And now, having had the experience, I knew exactly what to expect. I left the office with an appointment for the exam on my twenty-first birthday, April 17, 1973.

I stayed that night once again at the Motel 6 that had just been built in Joliet. It was a very nice facility and the first of the new economy lodging choices just coming on line at the time. It really did cost only $6.60 a night. I decided the next morning to head for the union hall to see if I could ship out on another towboat for a couple of weeks before heading home to study. At this point I had rented a dinky little house across from the baseball park in Prescott. Fully equipped with secondhand everything direct from Goodwill. I was a regular employee with Twin City Barge then, and I wanted as many *accrued days off* paid to me as possible.

accrued days off - Twin City Barge provided one day off with pay for each day that an employee worked aboard their towboats.

My hope was that when I told them I'd gotten my license, my being *out of days* would improve my chances to considered for a pilothouse position.

The next morning at the union hall, a cook's job for Material Service was posted at the first call of the morning at 9:00 a.m. There was a second call that morning and another in the afternoon, but nothing else came in. At the end of the day, I was considering what to do.

"George, would you give me that cook's job?"

George looked at me and paused for a time. "Struve! Can you cook?"

"As good as the next guy. I worked in a restaurant for years growing up in Wisconsin."

"Look," he said, "git yourself some white t-shirts and a cookbook. Do a respectable job! I don't wanna hear nothin' bad about this!"

So the next morning, I got on the MV *Alfred A. Hagerty*, a Material Service boat, at their home office in Lockport. I did go and purchase two packages of white t-shirts and a cookbook before I went.

MV *Alfred A. Hagerty*, Material Service towboat.

out of days - when an employee used up all their accrued days off

I had observed towboat cooks all the years I'd worked on towboats, and frankly, the job looked easy. Most of them appeared about 4:30 a.m. in the galley and hit the sack again right after breakfast. Another appearance late in the morning lasting through lunchtime, and once dishes were done and things cleaned up, the cook disappeared again till late afternoon.

They started getting dinner around 4:00, 4:30 p.m. and were never in the galley later than 7:00 p.m. It looked like a racket to me. How nice would it be to sleep through an entire night on a towboat?

Photo of deckhands installing rigging on a tow.

It didn't take long for me to learn that cooking for a crew on a towboat was anything but a walk in the park. The *Hagerty* had a deck crew of four, an engineer, an oiler, the captain, and the pilot. The towboat had a generous galley and a commercial kitchen that was a joy to work in. Every tool you could desire, and the prior cooks had everything stocked up well.

My daily breakfast menu for my crew of eight included three pounds of pork sausage and at least three pounds of bacon. I would also make hash browns or American fries, fresh baking powder biscuits, and sausage gravy each day. Eggs to order always, and either hot grits or oatmeal on the side.

Once breakfast was done, I would do the baking for the day. Most days I made at least two pies plus a cake with homemade frosting or cupcakes. Emulating my favorite towboat cooks, I made hot, deep-fried, raised glazed donuts a couple times a week.

I started a roast (beef or pork) around 10:00 a.m. with potatoes, onions, etc., on the side to prepare for lunch. At least one homemade soup or chili each day and again biscuits or hot, fresh-baked bread for the midday meal. Always lots of salads and dressings and all the trimmings. About ten pounds of potatoes per day were peeled and boiled, and heaping portions of mashed potatoes and gravy were always available.

Dinner was a combination of leftovers and some main hot dish, lasagna or the like. This crew liked my spaghetti a great deal, so I served that every few days. Again, several vegetable and potato choices with each meal and hearty servings of the rich, hot comfort food. Throughout the day I also made sure that the outsized service refrigerator that faced the galley was stocked with cold cuts, cheeses, relishes, pickles, crackers, and all manner of eat-on-the-go food for between meals.

After a few days I did get the work streamlined to where I could get a short break between meals. I did not, however, learn to do all this work as quickly or efficiently as the professionals I had watched over the years. It was very rewarding, and the first week flashed by.

About eight days in I sensed something was amiss. The friendly atmosphere had faded a bit, and the crew seemed a little sour. The mate, John Cullen, and I were pals from a long time back.

"John, do you know what's going on with the crew here? All the sudden, I'm kinda gitten' the cold shoulder from everybody."

John thought for a moment before answering. "You know, it might be that Dilly is tellin' everybody that you're leavin' soap on your dishes. He's got the shits, and he thinks you ain't rinsing them well enough."

"Well, that's a bunch of crap. The commercial sink has a temp gauge that shows the water coming out is boiling, and I rinse the heck out of everything. You know what it is? It's those damn beans he has me make for him. That's all he eats for lunch every day when he gets up to come on watch. It's a wonder he hasn't shit his brains out!"

The second day I was aboard as cook on the *Hagerty*, Dilly, the second mate, came into the galley. He was an enormous man. Six foot four and at least 400 pounds. He was not fat, just BIG. He gave me one of his friendly, semi-toothless smiles and asked if I would make him beans. He said most cooks loved to make them for him.

"Not sure how to do that, Dilly. Do you know what's in the recipe?"

Dilly opened one of the pantry doors and pulled out a package of dry Great Northern beans. "Ya jist take all the leftover breakfast everything and toss it in a pot with sliced onions, a package of beans, and some water and boil that all morning long."

I did as he asked and immediately increased the daily offerings of sausage and bacon to have even more left over for the bean feast. This new concoction was *really* good. I was proud of my first and only authentic Southern-style offering. Dilly loved it. He ate three or four enormous serving bowls full with bread and butter every day when he got up for lunch for several days in a row.

We discussed his eating habits the next time he came to the galley.

"Dilly, I heard through the grapevine that you're telling folks I'm leaving soap on the dishes. It ain't soap on the dishes that's causing your bathroom problems. Look in the kitchen. Water that hot, you ain't

155

having soap on the dishes. You just gotta cut back on the beans, man. Maybe just one bowl at a meal?"

Thankfully, Dilly agreed that I might have discovered the source of his loose bowels. He pleaded with me to continue making the beans each morning, stating over and over that they were the best he'd ever had.

Twenty days after getting aboard I was on my way home, understanding much more about how hard a cook's job on a towboat was. I had one week to hit the books all day, every day to get ready for the retake of my captain's license test. I only had that one section to redo, so I would focus harder on this than anything before in my life. I was determined and very confident that I could pass the remainder of the exam.

Just a few days away from fulfilling a major life goal.

"How did you get your first pilot job?"

"I was issued my First-Class Pilot License at the U.S. Coast Guard Office in Chicago on my 21st birthday, April 17, 1973. I contacted my employer and let them know. They put me to work as a pilot the following Monday morning."

Chapter 17

Hello, Jack. Yes, I Got My License.

"Good Morning, Twin City Barge, Lemont."

"Good morning. Jack Moore, please."

"Please hold for a moment. Let me see if he is in."

This was it. I had dreamt of making this phone call for a long time, and it was finally that long-awaited day.

"Jack Moore here."

"Good morning, Jack. It's Tom Struve. How're you doing today?"

"Tom Struve! How are you, sir? I was just lookin' at my list this morning and noticing that you are just about out of days. Didn't you all jist git some snow up there?"

"Yeah, we got a little Tuesday, but it all melted yesterday."

Company towboat MN *Viking* pushing tow of empty barges upbound through harbor in Downtown St. Paul, Minnesota.

"Well, you probably wanna go back to work, huh?"

"Yes, sir. But I have some news. I got my license Tuesday down in Chicago. I am now the proud owner of a ***1,000-ton First Class Pilot License.***"

1,000 ton First Class Pilot License - License classification for captain at that time. The largest towboats in existence then were the MV *United States* and the MV *America*, both quadruple-screw 9,000 horsepower and a little over 900 tons, so I requested 1,000 tons as my limit.

"Wow! Congratulations, Tom! I didn't know you were that far along. I know you had a steering letter from us and all but didn't know you were getting that close."

"Yep. My last trip down there on the *Pawnee*, Larry Hetrick let me steer every afternoon for three weeks. I was on the front watch, and it worked out great. I think I'm ready, Jack."

Author as young pilot on one of Twin City Barge towboats.

"Let me call you right back, Tom. Got a couple of other calls here."

I was elated and anxious all at the same time. Lots of deck guys had steering letters, but I hadn't seen anyone advance to pilot since I had been with Twin City. There were no guarantees, but I had a strong hope they would let me give it a try.

Jack called back about ten long minutes later. "Tom, here's the deal. We have all sorts of folks who claim they want to be pilots for us, but they just talk a big stick—they don't get their license. You made this happen, and that says a lot about you. What if I ask you to show up this coming Monday morning at St. Paul at the **wharf barge** and get on the *Santee* as pilot?

"We're just **shipping her up**, and you can go out on her first trip of the season up there. Clair Marks will be the captain, and you will be the pilot. Okay with you?"

Okay with me? Are you kidding me!? Okay with me?! It took me a couple of seconds to get my breath back. Apparently, I had been holding it.

"Heck yes, Jack. I will be happy to be there. Wow. I am super grateful you're givin' me this chance. I know I will be a good pilot for you. I won't let you down."

I hung up the phone, stunned at this new reality, and let it sink in. I had made it. I was going into the pilothouse. My dream since I was a little guy. I couldn't wait for Monday to arrive. I said an earnest prayer of thanks acknowledging this fortuitous opportunity and opened my front door into a great, sunshine-filled day.

wharf barge - a waterside resource center operated by the towboat company where towboats come for minor repairs and to take on supplies and fuel, etc.

shipping her up - A towboat is *shipped up* when the crew arrives, and she goes into service and **laid up** when she is secured, and the crew is sent home.

Chapter One from
PILOTHOUSE DAYS

"Tell me about those first days and weeks as a new pilot and then a captain."

"I was in heaven. At every turn I was blessed with opportunity. I had excellent crews, superior equipment, and I was a quick learner. The company showed great confidence in me by promoting me to captain after only ninety days."

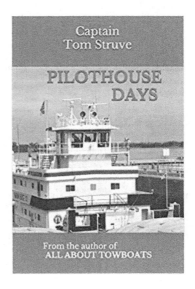

Captain
Tom Struve

PILOTHOUSE
DAYS

From the author of
ALL ABOUT TOWBOATS

1. Getting Ready to Go Around

"I think they are gonna pass by *on the one*."

We were completing our overnight *orders*, moving one loaded barge down to Twin City's barge fleets near South St. Paul. We'd left the ADM (Archer Daniels Midland) barge-loading facility minutes before and were traveling downbound just upstream from downtown St. Paul, Minnesota, on the Mississippi River. Most of the lovely bright yellow and orange leaves on the softwood trees lining the Mississippi had already succumbed to October freezes and subsequent windy rainstorms. Bald eagle sightings are frequent

orders – slang expression describing direction given to the boat crews by dispatchers. Typically, each morning and afternoon, company officials (most commonly called "dispatchers") provide a list of "orders" or directions about what barges to move and/or where to go.

along this leisurely stretch of the river, with a state park on the ***right bank*** and an old industrial riverfront on the ***left bank***.

My ***steersman***, Jimmy Svoboda, was leaning forward, watching intently over the pilothouse console on the *Mallard*. The approach or position

MV *Julie White*, formerly MV *Lindholm*.
Sister and copy of MV *Mallard*.
Telescopic pilothouse. Twin screw, 2,000 horsepower.

of any ***pleasure craft*** forward of your tow always merits some concern. I seldom got too worked up about it. I was enjoying sitting on the rear bench of the pilothouse in the love seat-type arrangement with a pillow behind my lower back and a big glass of ice water next to me.

"You know, I used to work with a pilot named Whitey Fleshman. He had serious concerns about pleasure boats passing near our tow. I really felt sorry for him. He musta run somebody over somewhere along the way. Whenever a pleasure boat came into view, even a long way off, he would jump out of his chair, lean over the sticks, pull back the throttles, and just agonize.

right bank – The right bank is always the right side of a river, moving downstream. This important designation helps to communicate where something is located or where boats might travel or pass one another.
left bank – The left bank is always the left side of a river, moving downstream.
steersman – a person learning how to steer a towboat
pleasure craft – motorboats, canoes, sailboats used for recreation

"Which way you think they're gonna go?' he'd shout. He did that every time a boat came on the horizon in front of him. Canoe, cabin cruiser. Didn't make any difference. He was a super nice guy. I wish I'd asked him why he was so anxious all the time. Just seemed a shame."

"Should I blow them a whistle?" Jimmy asked.

"I wouldn't unless you get in a really tight spot with them. I can't tell you how many times I tried when I started out as a pilot to follow the Rules of the Road and blow a whistle when a pleasure craft was coming at me. Almost without exception, Jimmy, all it does is screw them up. The moment they hear that whistle, they seem to assume they must be doing something wrong, and frankly, too many dang times they change course, most times dangerously. You try it if you want. You see if I'm not right. Too many times they do something really stupid."

The Rules of the Road are the official guidelines governing every boat on the water. Raft or canoe to the biggest tow or ship around. There is a rule or two for every passing or encounter. The rules include who has the *right of way* and who is *burdened*.

"Jimmy, do you have all the rules memorized yet?"

"Yeah. Pretty much. It took me the longest time to git *one whistle* or *two whistle* and *ascending* or *descending* straight. Jist like when I was first deckin'. Trying to get the red and green running lights straight. I always had to look back from the head of the tow to see the lights on the top outside corners of the pilothouse, and then I'd see which way to put 'em."

Jimmy was a good steersman. Not the best pilot I had the opportunity to train, but not the worst. Southern Minnesota farm boy. Giant hands callused from

right of way – When passing or overtaking another vessel, one of the vessels has priority and selects how passing or overtaking will occur.
burdened – In a right of way scenario, the burdened vessel has the least ability to maneuver. Example, a sailboat is almost always the burdened vessel in contrast to any boat that has propulsion.
one whistle – overtaking with the other boat to your left
two whistle – overtaking with the other boat to your right
ascending – traveling upstream
descending – traveling downstream

from years of hard work. Modest dresser. Always in a plaid long sleeve shirt. Mutton chop sideburns, mostly unkempt. Brown hair, bright blue eyes, prominent German nose, lots of nose hair. About six foot two, same as me, but a lot more muscle. Hailed from Kenyon, Minnesota, a town of about 1,800 on the Zumbro River. His dad managed the co-op feed store there, and Jimmy was throwing bags of feed and fertilizer into the beds of pickups before he could see up inside the box. He came from a family of ten kids. Seven brothers, two sisters. Big family reunion each fall, held at the Lutheran church cemetery, coinciding with the annual Kenyon Rose Fest.

Most of his classmates opted for trade schools after high school or became working partners on the family farm. Jimmy met a guy named Steamboat Bill at a bar while staying with his cousin over the 4th of July in Newport, Minnesota. His new pal worked on the river and told him how jobs were easy to get, and the work was OK. Jimmy stopped at the address Bill gave him, and they hired him on the spot. He drove home to Kenyon, grabbed his work clothes, and said goodbye to very concerned parents.

"You be damn sure to always have clean underwear on, case you gotta go to the hospital," his mother warned.

"Do they give you a life vest?" his dad asked.

Drove me crazy that he refused to buy a decent pair of sunglasses. "Jimmy, I am gonna git pissed if you don't listen to me about this. There might not be a more hostile environment for that one set of eyeballs that you own than staring out onto the water from this pilothouse day after day. I can't see a dang thing out of your sunglasses because they have so many scratches! What in the world are you thinking, man!?" I was teasing, but in fact, I was very concerned.

"I know. I know. Next time I git uptown, I'm gonna git me some good ones. Maybe some of them polarized jobs."

I felt honored that Twin City Barge repeatedly put steersmen with me. Many of these pilots in training were enthusiastic and wanted to learn, listen, and do well. Occasionally, despite their intense desire, some student pilots simply lacked the natural ability and skill to succeed. They could learn, but it would never come easy or be very pretty. Trying to teach folks who lacked natural ability could be trying.

164

I liked working with Jimmy. He was about midway between really skilled and sort of skilled. But he reeeally wanted to learn. He had a great attitude, always a friendly smile, and a huge, easy laugh. He'd gotten on the *Mallard* two days earlier. They put him with us, knowing that we were **going around**, over to Chicago, and thought that seeing the entire Upper Mississippi all the way to St. Louis downstream from St. Paul and then the entire Illinois River going upstream to our Chicago area fleet and office would be good for him. Jimmy would show glimpses of true natural skill and ability from time to time. I had a good feeling about that young man. He was grateful to be aboard and clearly understood the value of this opportunity.

The natural ability part of being a towboat pilot can be explained like this: With a bit of common sense and some time around towboats and barges, most people can get **between the sticks** and get up or down the river. What differentiates good pilots and captains from average or not so good is the ability to see yourself getting into trouble before you are too far gone to recover. It is just that simple.

Here's another way to explain it. Folks in towboat pilothouses with great natural ability have an inherent sense (born with it — you either have it or you don't) of spatial geometry. Whether navigating upstream or down, you are constantly envisioning *your tow* in the space immediately ahead of you and lots of times you need to steer in a way that gives you room to get the tow through that next space.

Not long after I became a pilot at Twin City Barge, the management there recognized my natural aptitude and leadership gifts and arranged whenever possible for me to be a captain on their towboats. I ran a good towboat. I was an accomplished and personable pilot, and it wasn't long before I gained a reputation among my fellow captains and the deck crews of being fun, fair, and highly skilled. On towboats where I was captain, everyone enjoyed working hard, and we got a lot done. We did things rapidly and efficiently and

going around – Twin City Barge had operations in both the St. Paul and Chicago Harbors. In the spring and fall they would shift towboats from one location to the other. We called it "going around" because you would travel the Mississippi to St. Louis and then go up the Illinois or the reverse.
between the sticks – Towboats do not have steering wheels. The captain steers with levers called "sticks" mounted on the console in the pilothouse. There is a set of sticks for each set of rudders, steering rudders and backing rudders. Steering rudders are used going forward, and backing rudders are used to steer in reverse.
your tow – one or a group of barges, steered from behind.

earned a healthy respect from other crews. It was one of my first major lessons in managing people. I saw over and over that people love being on the winning team. People love being part of the most successful group. People thrive when challenged to do better than average and love to be recognized as the best. The varsity team.

***

Towboat season in St. Paul was about to end. November brings seriously cold temperatures at night and stretches of chilly, silver-sky days when farmers hurry to get the last of the row crops gathered from fields and into storage. Every barge company rolls the dice to get one more tow downbound out of St. Paul just in the nick of time to avoid getting frozen in. The massive grain depots where barges are loaded work around the clock during those fall harvest months, making that last big push.

"We are not getting out of here one day too soon, Jimmy. S'posed to dip down to five degrees tonight. The deckhands have been super careful not to get lines wet for days now 'cause they're no good when it freezes overnight. Wet, frozen line is too stiff to tie up a barge."

Jimmy looked back at me. "This is about the time they always take their boats around, right?"

I nodded. "Everybody says you need to be southbound no later than Thanksgiving. A cool, wet fall causing the water temps to dip and a robust early winter storm with subzero temps for only a day or two will lock up Lake Pepin bad. Two years ago an ADM tow got stuck in Lake Pepin. They hammered and hammered, determined to get through. Punched a bunch of holes in the lead barges and finally gave up. They had crews up here all winter long tending to pumps. Didn't get the barges out of the middle of the lake till spring."

"Holy crap. I didn't know that. Well, I can't wait to get headed south. If we git a lot of ice, won't some of the buoys git moved out of place? I am really hoping when I'm steering to see them all where they're s'posed to be, so I can make good notes in my *river charts.*"

"We should be OK, Jimmy. Comin' back upriver in the spring is when you see all the buoys moved or missing because of the winter ice. That

river charts – In the days before technology-augmented mapping, captains and pilots used river charts like we used to use road maps. They often made personal notes in the charts about navigating in challenging areas, which others would find valuable. Photo on page 20.

is when it pays to have been back and forth here enough times that you know where to run without buoys. I've made the upbound spring trip for Twin City for the past six years, and we always seem to pass the northbound **buoy tender** down around Hannibal or somewhere like that. From there, all the way to St. Paul, you just feel your way along. Worse than buoys being missing is that lots of them have been moved **off station** by the ice. You gotta watch super careful with your charts to be sure where you are running. You almost gotta pretend that the buoys you see aren't there."

***

The day before, we were in at the **wharf barge** taking on fuel. Upon a large old flat-deck construction barge, Twin City Barge had constructed a metal warehouse with a machine shop and mechanics' area inside the up-stream half. There were lockers for equipment and storage accessible with a forklift on the other half. The floor was seasoned blacktop, and rolls of line and spools of flexible steel cable were stacked opposite the locked door of the storage area that held sundry supplies like bedding, towels, batteries, mops, brooms, and the like for their towboats. The wharf barge was held in place by long sloping steel tubes on each end and the wood-planked truck-access ramp. These movable connections to shore allowed the entire stationary floating unit to move up and down, depending on **the stage of the river**.

I walked up the ramp, which smelled of **creosote** and fuel and every-thing spilled on it over the years. Just past the modest parking area at the edge of this man-made levee, I entered the nearest of the Twin City Barge offices to say hi to the dispatchers. Ed Williams, John Schwab, and the head dis-patcher, Bob Jorgens. The dispatch center was one big room with fluorescent lights and multiple magnetic whiteboards covered with dozens of one-inch-by-two-inch magnets. Each magnet had a crayon-applied number and repre-sented a barge in one ofthe many fleets. It was fun to see that office environment, phones ringing and men in shirts and ties. So different from the

---

buoy tender – The US Coast Guard operates special towboat-barge units complete with a crane. They carry lots of navigation buoys and equipment and travel along rivers fixing navigation aids that need attention. Photo on page 20.

off station – a river buoy that has gotten moved from where it is supposed to be

wharf barge – a barge secured to the bank of a river that serves as a mooring station, supply depot, repair shop, etc.

stage of the river – "Stage" is the water level above some arbitrary point, usually with the zero height being near the river bed. "Flood stage," for instance, is the stage at which a river will overflow its banks.

creosote – an acrid solution used to treat timbers and wooden poles like pilings and telephone poles to keep them from rotting; banned as a carcinogen around 2005.

on-the-water-aboard-the-towboat working portion of this business. The dispatchers liked me, and I liked them. I like to think I was one of their favorites.

"I gotta tell ya, Jimmy, I was tickled when Bob told me about our tow. They're giving us two loads and six empties for this trip going around. What a breeze. And then the empties turned out to be *hoppers* — no stacked covers. Man! And, I think Bob said we go all the way through to St. Louis with this tow. Somebody here is living right, I can tell you that!

"Yer gonna like steering the way we arranged our tow, Jimmy. Way better than if we woulda made it a *knockout single*. We'll be so much closer to the head of the tow, and the two loads made up as a *unit tow* will let us scoot right along. This is gonna be a nice trip."

It was 11:30 a.m. We had just arrived at one of Twin City's *lower fleets*, and we *topped the loaded barge around* before placing it in the *starboard* bow corner location, finishing off a tow of fifteen loads for the waiting *line-haul towboat* called the MV *American Beauty*.

"The *Beauty* to the *Mallard*, come in on channel seven."

"Go ahead there, Captain," I responded after switching marine radio channels.

"Man! We ain't gittin' outta here one minute too soon! I don't know how you all put up with this cold. I can't stop shiverin'!"

"I hear ya. We are gonna be right behind you guys southbound
in a couple days, headin' over to Chicago. Hopefully, we all will make it

hoppers – open container barges without covers used to haul materials not needing protection from weather
knockout single - the tow can be locked in one single locking if you unfasten the towboat from the tow and move it into the notch in the tow.
a unit tow – a group of barges arranged with rakes (round, sloping ends) on each end so you can go faster
lower fleets – In the St. Paul/Minneapolis Harbor these were the fleets farthest downstream. "Fleets" are spaces along the river with moorings along the shore where barges are temporarily stored.
topped the barge around – turn the barge 180 degrees and go the other direction
starboard – the right side of the boat or the tow
line-haul towboat – A line-haul towboat is typically larger (between two and ten-thousand horsepower). Most are live-aboard and tow larger numbers of barges long distances, St. Louis to St. Paul, for instance. Photo on page 21.

168

through these larger *pools* on the upper end without too much ice!"

"Well, maybe we'll see you down the line. Thanks for bringin' us this last barge. We'll be southbound as soon as they turn me loose."

"Ten-four. Good luck to you. If we don't talk on the way out, we'll see you up here next year." I hung the microphone back on the console. It was close to lunch and an afternoon nap. Frank Rhymer was our pilot and about to come up and take over the helm of the *Mallard*.

"Are you gonna steer for Frank too, Jimmy?" I asked.

"Heck, yes! All I can. He said he would be happy for me to steer some for him. I hope to grab just a quick catnap late in the day and git some good night running experience with both of you if you'll let me."

"Frank is really good, Jimmy. Pay close attention to what he shares with you. He used to work over on line-haul towboats for Mobil Oil. Unit tows all over the place. He is one of the best I have ever seen."

As captain on the *Mallard*, I was on the *forward watch*. Frank Rhymer, our pilot, worked the *after watch*. Frank and I really liked each other and worked together occasionally. I loved working on Twin City's towboats with him. Frank had a great Southern sense of humor and loved to visit. Stories, stories, and more stories.

The pilothouse, mounted on *telescopic slides*, moved a bit as Frank, with his perpetual toothpick in his mouth, walked up the port stairway. "Good morning, Tommy! How you doin', Jimmy? Staying outta trouble?" Jimmy slid out of the pilothouse chair, and Frank moved in front of the controls.

"I am finer than frog's hair, Frank! Captain Struve here is sure enough keeping me outta trouble! All the time! I can't believe how lucky I am to be

pools – When the Army Corps of Engineers installs locks and dams on a river, the water that backs up behind them is called a "pool." In some areas the pools are very wide, extending bank to bank.
forward watch – 6 a.m. to noon, and 6 p.m. till midnight
after watch – noon till 6 p.m. and midnight to 6 a.m.
telescopic slides – Some towboats are built so the pilothouse can move up and down utilizing a hydraulic hoist. These boats can navigate under low bridges.

getting to steer for you two while we go around. I hit the towboat lottery jackpot!"

"Well, you two git down there and belly up to the table. Johnny's got his best Sunday fried chicken and all the fixin's. I can't back away from the table when I'm on a boat that he's on. They're gonna have to pick me off here with a crane when we git to Chicago. I'll be such a tub!"

I laughed and handed the clipboard with the orders to Frank as he took over the controls. "Grab six empties around the corner across from the wharf barge going to the Port Cargill Fleet. There's only about a dozen barges left back there, so it should be easy to git them together. The *Viking* made us a tow of six loads. We will grab and bring them down and set them up as the first six in the next loaded downbound line-haul tow. Looks like we'll be doing the scramble up the Minnesota and back for a day or two and then head south with two loads and six empties. I got 'em all set up and the tow almost completely built in the upper corner of the Packing House Fleet. Had a little time this morning while we were waiting on orders."

"Boy, I can't wait to git pointed southbound. You guys are crazy, you know that, Tommy!? Your brains is froze! I 'bout froze damn to death last night. Had two heaters goin' up here, and Bill had to loan me his heavy jacket. How in the hell do you live up here? And don't you own one of those snow machines? What in the hell? I can't believe anybody'd go outdoors when it gits like this. I am tellin' you, your brains is all froze! That's what it is!" Frank adjusted the rudders as we turned and headed around the corner to get our empties.

"You Southern boys are sooooo soft, Frank! Ha! This isn't anything. Just some nice crisp fall weather. Hopefully, we won't get that snow they're talkin' about tonight. If the ground gits covered with snow, the temp can really go down."

"Well, go on and git yourself some grub. When you come back up to steer, Jimmy, I kin sit back here in back a' ya and sun myself like a turtle on a log. Maybe warm damn up a little bit! You people are crazy, livin' here. Just plain crazy!"

Jimmy and I laughed as we walked down the pilothouse stairway and astern toward the galley. Both of us were born and raised in the Midwest, so we took the ribbing about our winters completely in stride.

170

"Frank sure is a good egg, isn't he?"

"And like I was telling you, Jimmy, git all the time with him you can on this trip. Don't be afraid to ask questions. Ask him if you can copy his notes from his river charts if he has them along. He is really good, and you can learn a lot from him."

The aroma from the galley was intoxicating.

"Johnny! I heard you got your Sunday best fried chicken! I am hungry. Let's eat, Jimmy!"

Pilothouse view of tow on the Mississippi River.

Upper Mississippi River & Illinois Waterway

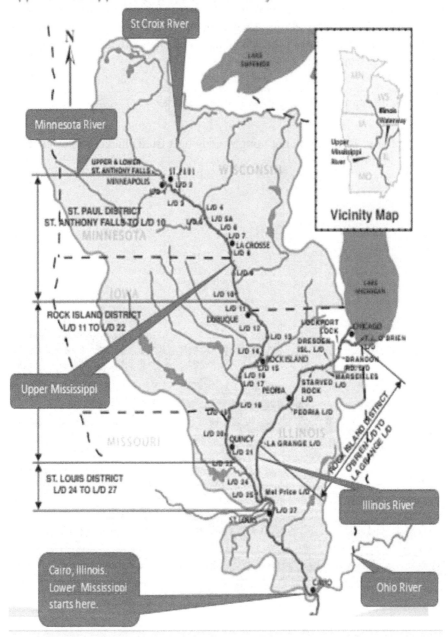

Appendix

Map Page 10-Locks and Dams, From Water Resources Planning for the Upper Mississippi River and Illinois Waterway, Public Domain. U.S. Army Corp of Engineers.

Photo Page 19- File: Prescott, Wisconsin Bridge Spanning St. Croix River.jpg From Wikipedia Commons; Public Domain. Photo taken August 1st, 1989.

Photo Page 22- Confluence of Mississippi and St. Croix Rivers at Prescott, Wisconsin. Used by permission of photographer Dallas Eggers from Prescott, Wisconsin. (drone)

Photo Page 24-FileHistoricdowntown.jpg. From Wikipedia Commons; Public Domain. Photo taken March 16, 2004, by James Stinson.

Photo Page 28- Leo's Landing. Used with permission of owner, Janice Anderson.

Photo Page 29- LIFT SPAN, SOUTH SIDE, LOOKING NORTH -Prescott Bridge, Spanning St. Croix River on U.S. Highway 10, Prescott, Pierce County, Wisconsin. Library of Congress, HAER WIS, 47 -PRES.V,1--13

Photo Page 32- Prescott Bridge, Spanning St. Croix River on U.S. Highway 10, Prescott, Pierce County, WI. Historic American Engineering Record, Creator, et al., photographer by Levy, Burt. Retrieved from the Library of Congress, https://www.loc.gov/item/wi0233/.

Photo Page 36- File Aerial view of Prescott Bridge and BNSF Railway bridge over St. Croix River. Photo taken May 18, 2010.

Photo Page 40-Common Carp.jpg. From Wikipedia Commons; Public Domain. Common Carp in Lake Powell. Photo by Leonard G, May 2006.

Photo Page 42- MV *Sioux* at Prescott, Wisconsin. Used by permission of owner, Dallas Eggers from Prescott, Wisconsin.

Photo Page 45 – Lemont Area, From videos, File: YouTube, Marktwained, River Captain Kyle Pfenning. Hundreds of awesome towboat videos at https://www.youtube.com/user/marktwained.com

Photo Page 46- MV *Albert E. Heekin*. Used by permission of Richard Dunbar, Dick's Towboat Gallery. Photo taken by Dan Owen.

Photo Page 47-MV *Dresden*. Photo taken by author.

Photo Page 48-MV *Katheryn Beesecker,* formerly *MV WS Rhea.* Used by permission of Richard Dunbar, Dick's Towboat Gallery. Photo taken by Mark Haury.

Photo Page 51- Main Engines, From videos, File: YouTube, Marktwained, River Captain Kyle Pfenning. Hundreds of awesome towboat videos at https://www.youtube.com/user/marktwained.com

Photo Page 61-File a5k022.jpg. From Wikipedia Commons; Public Domain. Towboat MV *Bruce Darst* upbound at Clark Bridge, Louisville, Kentucky. Photo taken November 16, 2005, by William Alden III.

Photo Page 68 - MV *George W Lenzie.* Used by permission of Richard Dunbar, Dick's Towboat Gallery. Photo taken by Dan Owen.

Photo Page 74- Deckhand, Line, From videos, File: YouTube, Marktwained, River Captain Kyle Pfenning. Hundreds of awesome towboat videos at https://www.youtube.com/user/marktwained.com

Photo Page 76-MV *Albert E. Heekin.* Used by permission of Richard Dunbar, Dick's Towboat Gallery. Photo taken by Dan Owen.

Photo Page 89-Under Interstate 80. Image PNG IL 79 fhwa 1964, 568.JPG. MWRDGC modified by CDMO: \weisenberger\UAA (http://www.chicagoareawaterways.org/documents/CAWS-UAA-DRAFT-REPORT.pdf) Richard Weingrof, Office of Infrastructure.

Photo Page 91-MV *Brandon.* Used by permission of Richard Dunbar, Dick's Towboat Gallery. Photo taken by Dan Owen.

Photo Page 92-MV *AM Thompson.* Used by permission of Richard Dunbar, Dick's Towboat Gallery. Photo taken by Mark Haury.

Photo Page 93-MV *Marilyn Banta.* Used by permission of Richard Dunbar, Dick's Towboat Gallery. Photo taken by Don Grot.

Photo Page 97-Havana, Illinois, coal transfer facility, The Midland Story, C & IM Railroad, 1964.

Photo Page 105-Captain Steve Grossarth. Used by permission of Eric Grubb. Richard Dunbar, Dick's Towboat Gallery. Photo taken by Mark Haury.

Photo Page 109- MV *L. Wade Childress.* Used by permission of Richard Dunbar, Dick's Towboat Gallery. Photo taken by Don Grot.

Photo Page 116-MV *Northland.* Used by permission of Richard Dunbar, Dick's Towboat Gallery. Photo taken by Mark Haury.

Photo Page 118-MV *Ida Crown*. Used by permission of Richard Dunbar, Dick's Towboat Gallery. Photo taken by Mark Haury.

Photo Page 119- Material Service, From videos, File: YouTube, Marktwained, River Captain Kyle Pfenning. Hundreds of awesome towboat videos at https://www.youtube.com/user/marktwained.com

Photo Page 122-MV *Alfred Hagerty*. Used by permission of Richard Dunbar, Dick's Towboat Gallery. Photo taken by Mark Haury.

Photo Page 126-Montgomery Ward Catalogue House.JPG From Wikipedia Commons; Public Domain. Picture taken June 2007

Photo Page 131-MV *Kiowa*. Used by permission of Richard Dunbar, Dick's Towboat Gallery. Photo taken by George Reichardt.

Photo Page 134-MV *Manco*. Used by permission of Richard Dunbar, Dick's Towboat Gallery. Photo taken by Don Grot.

Photo Page 136-MV *Manco*. Used by permission of Richard Dunbar, Dick's Towboat Gallery. Photo taken by Don Grot.

Map Page 140-Chicagoriversystem.jpg. From Wikipedia Commons; Public Domain. Map of Chicago Sanitary Ship Canal and Cal-Sag Canal. Source: U.S. Geological Survey.

Photo Page 142-RobertStreetBridge2.jpg. From Wikipedia Commons; Public Domain. Picture taken March 2006

Photo Page 144- Heavy Ice, From videos, File: YouTube, Marktwained, River Captain Kyle Pfenning. Hundreds of awesome towboat videos at https://www.youtube.com/user/marktwained.com

Photo Page 146-NicholsRdConnectionatOldCedar_Ave_Bridge.jpg. From Wikipedia Commons; Public Domain. Picture taken June 1966.

Photo Page 152 -MV *Alfred A. Hagerty*. Used by permission of Richard Dunbar, Dick's Towboat Gallery. Photo taken by Mark Haury.

Photo Page 153 – Laying Rigging, From videos, File: YouTube, Marktwained, River Captain Kyle Pfenning. Hundreds of awesome towboat videos at https://www.youtube.com/user/marktwained.com

Photo Page 158 – File Towboat and Barges on the Mighty Mississippi.jpg. From Wikipedia Commons; Public Domain. Photo taken August 26, 2008, by Pete Markham.

Photo Page 162 - MV *Julie White*, sister and copy of *MV Mallard*. Used by permission of Richard Dunbar, Dick's Towboat Gallery. Photo taken by George Reichardt.

Photo Page 171- Tow on River, From videos, File: YouTube, Marktwained, River Captain Kyle Pfenning. Hundreds of awesome towboat videos at https://www.youtube.com/user/marktwained.com

Map Page 172 – Locks and the River; Boaters Guide to Safe Travel, US Army Corps of Engineers, http://www.mvr.usace.army.mil/Portals/48/docs/Nav/LocksAndRiver.pdf.

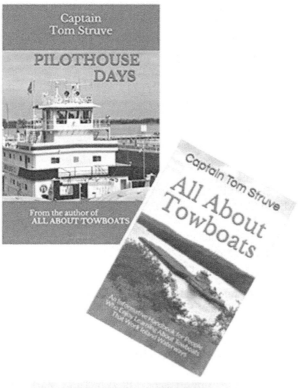

Be sure to get your copies of
the other two books in this series-
PILOTHOUSE DAYS

Made in the USA
Monee, IL
29 December 2020